MW01028816

FIRE
ON ICE

Darrell Davis
Foreword by Jordan Eberle

To Gord:
I still can't shake the memories
of showering in Indian Head. Did
we make any other bad road trips?

Darrell Davis

MacIntyre Purcell Publishing Inc.

FIRE

ON

ICE

Copyright 2013 Darrell Davis.

All rights reserved. No part of this book covered by the copyrights hereon may be reproduced or used in any form or by any means — graphic, electronic, or mechanical — without the prior written permission of the publisher. Any request for photocopying, recording, taping, or information storage and retrieval systems of any part of this book shall be directed in writing to the Canadian Reprography Collective, 379 Adelaide Street, West, Suite M1, Toronto, Ontario, M5V 1S5.

MacIntyre Purcell Publishing Inc.
194 Hospital Rd.
Lunenburg, Nova Scotia
B0J 2C0
(902) 640-2337

www.macintyrepurcell.com
info@macintyrepurcell.com

Printed and bound by Marquis.

Design: Channel Communications
Layout: Alexandra Hickey

Library and Archives Canada Cataloguing in Publication
Davis, Darrell, 1957–, author
Fire on ice : why Saskatchewan rules the NHL / Darrell Davis.
Issued in print and electronic formats. ISBN 978-1-927097-35-9 (pbk.).
--ISBN 978-1-927097-38-0 (epub).-- ISBN 978-1-927097-37-3 (pdf).
--ISBN 978-1-927097-36-6 (kindle)
1. Hockey--Saskatchewan--History. I. Title.

GV848.4.C3D39 2013   796.96209712'4   C2013-903152-9
C2013-903153-7

MacIntyre Purcell Publishing Inc. would like to acknowledge the financial support of the Government of Canada through Department of Canadian Heritage (Canada Book Fund) and the Nova Scotia Department of Tourism, Culture and Heritage.

MIX
Paper from responsible sources
FSC
www.fsc.org   FSC® C107923

DEDICATION
To my family and friends, some gone,
but all remembered...
— Darrell Davis

TABLE OF CONTENTS

FOREWORD

I started liking hockey at a young age. My parents, Lisa and Darren, told me I used to put on my socks and slide around on the linoleum floors, pretending that I was skating around, so they got me into organized hockey right away. My brother Dustin and I were out on the street all the time, playing hockey, sometimes with our sisters Whitney and Ashley. My grandparents were always helping, looking after me and letting me stay at their house when I played junior hockey for the Regina Pats after my parents had moved to Calgary. You look back at that now, those growing-up days in Regina, and realize that's where you started becoming a good hockey player, but at the time you didn't know that, you were just enjoying it because it was so much fun.

Things turn around pretty quickly. I've had tons of coaches. My dad was a big part of it, coaching me, and my mom was always driving me to the rink. There were coaches who realized I had a certain amount of skill and there's a huge, surrounding group in Regina who helped get you where you wanted to go. Coaches and other parents helped. There were summer teams to play on because hockey's such a big sport in Regina, in Saskatchewan, in Canada. Not only is it a great sport, but as you grow older you realize that's where you meet people and start making friends.

I'm a big fan of the game: I don't just love playing it, I love watching it. Hockey was my life. Still is. I'm a fan. I'm a stats fan. I probably know a lot of things that I don't really need to know. It's funny, I've known about so many guys and I've been meeting lots of Saskatchewan NHL guys, like Mike Sillinger and Brooks Laich. As soon as I play on a team I look to see who's from Saskatchewan. And I've never had a guy on a team from Saskatchewan who's a bad guy. Even for my fund-raising golf tournament you can get tons of guys to come from around Saskatchewan.

When my number was being retired by the Pats I started thinking about my whole career. I remember being drafted by the Pats when I was 16, a later pick, and I wasn't sure I was going to make it. I went to camp, had a great camp, and the rest is history. To be honest, if I wasn't drafted by the Pats I don't know if I would have gone to another junior team. I was a smaller guy so the college route seemed like a good way to go. But growing up watching the Pats, guys like Garth Murray and Matt Hubbauer, Jeff Friesen, I got a chance to play with them. I wanted to play for the Pats because I grew up watching them.

Then the Edmonton Oilers drafted me. That was kind of fluky, too, because they were always my favourite team. It was near the end of the first round, the 22nd pick, and I was kind of praying I would get picked by the Oilers. I wasn't sure it was going to happen, but I got lucky enough, got on the team at the right time, when they were in a rebuilding stage, and got to play for them right away. I was tied into the Oilers anyway because of growing up in Regina near Darrell Davis and his family, knowing about his dad (Lorne Davis, a late Oilers scout) and brother (Brad Davis, a current Oilers scout). Liane Davis, Darrell's sister, taught me how to skate! I grew up a big Oilers fan because Regina doesn't have an NHL team. I was drawn to the Oilers right away. I wasn't a Flames fan or a Jets fan, I hated the Maple Leafs. I used to watch Doug Weight and Ryan Smyth; they didn't have amazing stars at the time but I enjoyed watching them.

I'm a pretty avid reader. Most of the time I'm reading books about hockey, or about the mental side of the game. I like stuff like this book. I definitely wanted to read this book, to be involved with it, just like I wanted to read Ron MacLean's book about the heritage of hockey. I love books like that. I want to find out about the older guys. I know the game has changed a lot, so it's awesome when I hear stories from the olden days. Even the guys who used to play for the Oilers — MacT, Kevin Lowe and, obviously, Gretz — they talk about the olden days. And Gordie Howe is Mr. Hockey and he's from Saskatchewan! As funny as it sounds, Bryan Trottier, I think my grandma used to babysit him. I don't know if he remembered it, but my grandmother used to tell me that.

Saskatchewan is so small, well, it's pretty big in size, but not in population. And it's like one out of every two people I meet knows somebody I know and we're all connected somehow. Since I've been in the NHL my family has grown 1000 per cent!

Contributing this foreword to Darrell's book is a no-brainer. Hockey is a big part of my life, I have big ties to Saskatchewan, and if you can get the word out there, show the history of the game, maybe more kids will be involved. I know lots of kids already are involved, but the more kids who play hockey, the better. Hockey's a game I've been involved with a long time. Growing up I didn't think about it that much, but when I think back on it now it may have kept me away from getting into some bad things. The worst things we ever did was break a few windows from shooting pucks. I think Eva, Darrell's wife, replaced a few windows in their garage doors. I've met so many great people through hockey. Here's a perfect example: I can go to Regina and be involved with a charity golf tournament that raises $300,000 for the Hospitals Foundation of Regina. Things like that, it's pretty amazing to be a part of! Hockey's done that for me. Saskatchewan has done that for me. We grew up in Regina, five houses down from Darrell's family, went to school with Darrell's sons, Austin and Tanner, my brother and Tanner are great friends. Eva would keep on eye on us. Liane taught me how to skate! It's a family tie. That's how it works in Saskatchewan. You guys are a big part of where I am today.

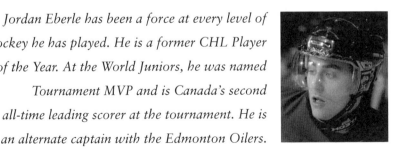

Jordan Eberle has been a force at every level of hockey he has played. He is a former CHL Player of the Year. At the World Juniors, he was named Tournament MVP and is Canada's second all-time leading scorer at the tournament. He is an alternate captain with the Edmonton Oilers.

PREFACE: IN SEARCH OF WENDEL CLARK

When I started writing this book about Saskatchewan hockey players, I had it in my mind that Wendel Clark was the prototypical player from the province: Grew up in the town of Kelvington, hard working, rugged, capable of scoring but never shied away from back-checking or aggressive play, fought when necessary and was a heart-and-soul member of his team. Just like Gordie Howe. Wendel Clark had to be in the book! Tiger Williams told me the same thing.

I started to track Clark when I visited Toronto for the 2012 Grey Cup. I called the Toronto Maple Leafs, who listed their former captain as an employee. I was told he didn't work in the Leafs office. So I sent an email to the person listed on-line as his representative, saying I wanted to interview Wendel for a book about NHL players from Saskatchewan, where they come from and why there are so many. No response. I went onto other research, always believing that I would eventually track down and interview Wendel Clark.

The original idea for this story came from Tom Maloney, former sports editor of the Globe and Mail. Tom lured me into freelancing for Canada's national newspaper by saying a great feature to write someday would be an article showing Saskatchewan as the heartland of the NHL. And I was the perfect guy to write it, having grown up in Saskatchewan as the son of an NHL player and long-time scout, Lorne Davis, and his wife, my mother Shirley, who may have been a better scout than my dad. I had all the connections from my earlier careers as a hockey official and sports writer, plus Edmonton Oilers star-in-the-making Jordan Eberle grew up just five houses away from my family's home in Regina.

To write the Globe story, I got press credentials for several Winnipeg Jets games — Thank you, Kalen Qually of the Jets staff! — and began conducting interviews. I started researching the article and sharing quotes with Al Maki, one of the Globe's excellent sports writers, who had talked to Saskatchewan-born NHLers like Patrick Marleau and Cory Sarich when they played in Calgary. As of this book's completion, the article had not appeared in the Globe and Mail. But a seed had been planted.

While Al and I were assembling a pretty good piece, which included my mid-winter road trip to Brooks Laich's home town of Wawota, John MacIntyre called me out of the blue. How he got my name and number, I still don't know. John's publishing company, MacIntyre Purcell, had success selling Saskatchewan-oriented books, so they wanted one written on hockey players from the Wheat Province. "Did you know Saskatchewan produces more NHL players per capita than any province, state or country?" I asked John. He had already figured that out. I was apparently the perfect guy to write the story because Saskatchewan guys relate to Saskatchewan guys, especially if you can talk about the Roughriders, the CFL team I covered for the Regina Leader-Post for more than two decades. As a publisher, John has been patient and understanding, plus he connected me with more good people, like editor Danny Gillis, promoter Alex Greek and layout maestro Alex Hickey. My former co-worker at the Leader-Post, Ian Hamilton, read every word and, as a good editor, chided me for making the same mistakes over and over. Danny caught every mistake, shortened the narrative when required, re-ordered some of my scattershot thoughts and, every time he sent me a revised chapter, made me look forward to reading the re-worked parts.

My sons, Austin and Tanner, were always encouraging and helpful. Their late mother, Eva, taught them how to leave me alone when I was writing and showed me how much I could accomplish if I would only sit down and concentrate. My friends from volunteer committees, hockey, football, media, and racquetball were inquisitive, supportive and understanding, especially my dear friend Susan Dauk, who shared the ups and downs of this process, would always ask "How's the book going?" and never failed to laugh at my "In Search of Wendel Clark" stories.

To turn the newspaper article into a book, I started by calling two of hockey's elder statesmen, both of whom had been teammates of my dad. I spoke to Elmer Lach, who was a linemate of Rocket Richard's and a teammate of my dad's in Montreal. He reminisced vividly about taking horse-drawn sleds to hockey games from his home town of Nokomis. Gordie Howe and my dad were teammates with the 1954–55 Red Wings, but because I couldn't talk to Gordie I spoke with his brother, Vic Howe, also a former NHLer, about making it to the big time and growing up with a legend.

I had already interviewed a number of Saskatchewan players for previous projects. I had spoken to Red Berenson, Clark Gillies, Jamie Heward and Eddie Litzenberger for an earlier book on the history of the Regina Pats. I had also chatted with Winnipeg Jets general manager and executive vice-president, Kevin Cheveldayoff, about his Saskatchewan roots, shortly after the team's joyous return to the Manitoba capital.

Many more interviews would need to be conducted, though. These were attempted with mixed success. I left a message for Johnny Bower. I sent notes to Ron Greschner's charity foundation about arranging an interview. I tried e-mailing Ron Delorme and Mike Sillinger. Mike responded after one of his charity events with Shooting Stars Foundation. Bernie Federko called back. Brian Propp and Orland Kurtenbach happily took my calls. I spent a long day following Jarret Stoll as he lugged the Stanley Cup to Neudorf and Yorkton. I met Tiger Williams for a beer, or two, or three — I bought every round and enjoyed every second of our animated conversation. I interviewed NHLers Luke and Brayden Schenn, Scott Hartnell, James Wright, Tanner Glass, Brooks Laich, Travis Moen, Chris Kunitz and Ryan Getzlaf on trips to Winnipeg. Unfortunately I missed Josh Harding, Darroll Powe, Nick Schultz and Braydon Coburn because, I learned, while NHL players are accessible after morning skates they are tough to corner following games for anything but stock quotes about that night's contest.

I called parents, relatives, coaches and volunteers and, when I crossed paths with somebody whose observations would fit into the book, I pulled out my digital recorder.

Everyone was co-operative and engaging. It's a Saskatchewan thing. I send them all my thanks.

I learned to go where hockey players went during the off-season. I met Glenn Hall, Fred Sasakamoose, Bryan Trottier and Marc Habscheid at the 2012 Saskatchewan Hockey Hall of Fame induction ceremony. I 'ran into' Tyler Bozak, Jaden Schwartz, Ryan Murray and Keith Aulie at golf tournaments. I spoke to Brett Clark, Blair Jones and Tanner Glass (again) following off-season workouts at the Regina hockey rink where my sister, Liane Davis, instructs them on power-skating and graciously arranged post-skate meetings. Devan Dubnyk and Jordan Eberle dropped into a golf tournament in Regina, where Eberle gave me his cell number so I could call him again, which I did several times. I also e-mailed him a few times when he was in Edmonton, plus once when he was competing in the world hockey championship in Stockholm, helping him through the unfamiliar process of writing the foreword for this book. He did it! Thanks, Ebs. You're a good guy from a good family and we had some great shinny games on our street.

After one of his workouts with Liane, Tanner Glass told me "When I was growing up, Wendel Clark was the guy I thought most Saskatchewan guys were like. I wanted to play like him."

"Wendel was here the other day," said Brett Clark (no relation) at the same Regina rink. "He was on his way to Wilcox because his son is going to play at Notre Dame."

Drat! Just missed him!

On the day I called the Maple Leafs office about Wendel Clark,

I later walked by the Hockey Hall of Fame in Toronto and fought an urge to head inside the entertaining, enthralling shrine because I had other work to do. Only later that night did I learn, from a Hall of Fame employee, that Clark had spent a couple hours inside the Hall that very day, visiting and signing autographs. "He's a great guy, you know?" said the employee, echoing what I had been told about Clark from everyone else. I was 200 feet away from him and didn't know it! A Toronto sports writer, after laughing at my near-miss, gave me Clark's cell phone number with this send-off: "Wendel's great, he'd love to talk about Saskatchewan." I kept putting off the call, not wanting to interrupt at the wrong time, and then realized "In this day and age, everyone uses electronic messaging. I'll text him!" I sent Clark a cryptic text about a book concerning Saskatchewan NHL players and said I would like to interview him.

I don't know if Clark got the text or not, but as the book progressed I realized I had enough information. Although Clark's input would have been great, I didn't need to talk to the prototypical NHL player from Saskatchewan because so many others I did speak to also fit the description. They all work hard. They're all approachable. They're all proud of where they come from. They all admire the other guys from Saskatchewan. They all remember who helped them get there.

There are nearly 50 Saskatchewan-born players in the NHL every year. About 500 have played in the NHL since its inception in 1917. Several data banks keep the list, but any published list almost immediately gets outdated because another Saskatchewanian is always about to join an NHL team. Each one deserves to be mentioned and honoured, simply because it's an amazing accomplishment, but there truly isn't enough space in one book to write about everyone. Hopefully the essence of Saskatchewan's NHL players is contained herein. And if Wendel Clark texts back someday, I'll see if I can add another chapter.

DARRELL DAVIS

July, 2013

Jarret Stoll played his minor hockey in Neudorf before moving on to play minor hockey in Melville and Yorkton.

BRINGING HOME
THE STANLEY CUP

After the Los Angeles Kings' sixth-game victory at home against the New Jersey Devils earned them the NHL's most coveted prize, the players celebrated on the town. They lugged the Stanley Cup to L.A.'s beaches and nightclubs and made the prerequisite stops on TV talk shows. But protocol also allows each member of the winning team to spend one day during the subsequent offseason with the 34-pound, silver trophy. Centre Jarret Stoll knew right away what he was going to do for his special day with the Cup.

"Me and my parents talked, me and my family, about what I'd want, they'd want," said Stoll. "We were all on the same page: bringing it to Neudorf, to Yorkton, and making it an all-day event."

When it was suggested that Neudorf, Saskatchewan, population 280, was the smallest community the Stanley Cup would visit, Stoll concurred.

"Yeah, probably, I couldn't imagine many smaller."

Neudorf is like most Saskatchewan communities — it has an

indoor hockey rink and it produces National Hockey League players. Ontario, Canada's most-populated province, produces the most NHLers every year — 203 in the lockout-shortened 2012–13 season, out of 921 players who got onto the ice for at least one NHL regular-season contest. But consider that Ontario has 13.4 million people. In an average season nearly 50 Saskatchewan-born players suit up with NHL teams from a population of only 1.06 million. This works out to 4.8 NHL players per 100,000 people. No other jurisdiction comes close — Manitoba is second at 2.6 players per 100,000 people

On the summer day in 2012 that the Cup came to Neudorf, a crew from the Saskatchewan Department of Highways was patching Highway 22, air-blasting rocks from potholes, spraying the cracks and indentations with oil, tossing in shovels of asphalt from a waiting truck and rolling them smooth with a massive roller. With its Co-Op food store and a credit union, the town sits just north of the picturesque Qu'Appelle Valley, about a two-hour drive northwest of Saskatchewan's capital city, Regina, on land so flat that all the standard jokes apply. Saskatchewan: Where it's so flat you can sit on your porch and watch your dog run away for three days. Whatya mean the earth is round? It looks flat from here!

A portable sign on Main Street read "Welcome Home Jarret Congratulations." Stoll stopped in on his grandmother before heading to the Weger Sports Complex, where a thousand fans waited for him. Gary Hoehn, the emcee for the festivities, kept jumping onto the flatbed truck that served as a makeshift stage to remind everyone that profits from the hamburger stand, beer gardens and sales of 50/50 tickets would go to the Jarret Stoll Patient Comfort Endowment Fund for Sick Children at Royal University Hospital in Saskatoon. Then Hoehn brought the hometown hero to the stage.

"I couldn't ask for anything more. To family, friends, the people of Neudorf and surrounding communities, it's very special to bring (the Stanley Cup) here," Stoll said.

"From the second I started playing hockey, learning to skate in that building right there, I wanted to win this big, shiny mug and bring it out here for you guys to enjoy. Thank you all for coming and enjoy the day... only in Neudorf, where the beer gardens open at 9 a.m.! I like that a lot!"

Everybody cheered and laughed.

After the speeches, Stoll was led to a tent, where fans had built a shrine to his career, complete with one of the first tiny jerseys he wore while playing in Neudorf. Here, shaded from the hot sun, Stoll posed one snapshot at a time beside the Stanley Cup with hundreds of well-wishers.

"I coached him," recalled Gary Hoehn, the emcee. "His dad, Tim, and I coached a team. It was probably novice, most of the kids were 6, 7 and 8. All country kids start skating young. With these little rinks you can skate all the time. He took the figure skating, the power skating. In the cities that doesn't happen: You can't put on your skates and walk to the rink. Here, you would phone the caretaker if you wanted to go down to the rink and he would say, 'OK, I'll turn off the lights when you're done.' My kid played with Jarret as they were growing up. Great kids. You hope you have a little input into their career, whether they know it or not.

I'm proud of him. As a coach I don't want too much. These kids weren't in the street causing a commotion. When they got home they were tired. The next day they were out again, not causing trouble. It didn't matter if you were the No. 1 player in town or the second one, they were all happy to play together."

Stoll's hockey career took him from Neudorf to Melville to Yorkton to Saskatoon, where he played in the elite Saskatchewan Midget AAA Hockey League. From Saskatoon he joined the Edmonton Ice of the Western Hockey League, until the junior team moved to Cranbrook, B.C., and became the Kootenay Ice. In 2002, Stoll was the Ice's captain when the team won the Memorial Cup as the best junior hockey team in Canada and the U.S. He also represented Canada at the world junior championships in 2001 and 2002, serving as team captain in his second stint when the Canadians won a silver to complement the bronze medal of one year earlier.

The Calgary Flames chose Stoll in the second round of the 2000 NHL entry draft, but he never signed with Calgary — although he nearly got traded to the Toronto Maple Leafs, who desperately wanted to sign him — and re-entered the draft in 2002. The Edmonton Oilers drafted him 36th overall, moving him through their farm system before he became a fulltime NHLer in 2005–06. That was the season they lost the Stanley Cup in a seventh-game heartbreaker to the Carolina Hurricanes. When he was traded to Los Angeles, two years later, it admittedly disheartened him for awhile, but he was a pivotal member of the Kings' championship march in the spring of 2012. Stoll's personal highlight during those playoffs came in Game 5 of the Western Conference final series, when he scored the overtime goal that eliminated the Vancouver Canucks, who had been odds-on favourites to win the Stanley Cup that year.

Two other NHLers have come from Neudorf: Brian Propp, who began a 15-year NHL career with the Philadelphia Flyers in 1979, and Eddie Litzenberger, a four time Stanley Cup winner, once as captain of the 1961 Chicago Blackhawks and three times as a Toronto Maple Leaf. Neudorf is also the home of a Nobel Prize winner. A small park sits beside Highway 22, with bushes and flowers and a bench, named in honour of Henry Taube. Born in Neudorf in 1915, Taube moved to Regina to attend Luther High School. After graduating from the University of Saskatchewan in Saskatoon, the province's biggest city, Taube became an instructor at the University of California-Berkeley and a leading researcher in chemical reactions. Taube, who died in 2005, won the 1983 Nobel Prize for chemistry.

"Henry Taube? He didn't play hockey!" Brian Propp said with a laugh. "I guess if you didn't play hockey you could put your nose into books, work very hard and be very intelligent, and accomplish things that don't take you to the NHL."

"We didn't have very much," said Propp about life in small town Saskatchewan."But we had all the values everybody grows up with, knowing how to work hard and not expect anything, to be a role model for others."

Brian Propp had 425 goals and 579 assists for 1,004 points in 1,016 regular-season NHL games. He also represented Canada internationally five times, playing 32 games and posting 20 points. In 160 NHL playoff games he scored 64 times and added 84 assists for 148 points. He advanced to the Stanley Cup finals in 1980, 1985 and 1987 with the Flyers, in 1990 with the Boston Bruins and in 1991 with the Minnesota North Stars. To Propp's dismay, his five trips to the Stanley Cup finals did not result in a Cup win. However, in true Saskatchewan form, he's respectful of the accomplishments of others.

"I thought Jarret Stoll played great in the playoffs, especially the finals," said Propp. "The great players play even better in those situations. I sent him a note after he won and I found out he was taking the Stanley Cup to Neudorf. I tried working it out but I couldn't get there. That was a great thing, taking it to Neudorf and Yorkton. I didn't win a Cup, I got there five times, which might make some people think less of me. But I see that I'm still in the top 30 in all the (NHL's scoring) categories and I believe I was a pretty good player, even though I didn't win a championship."

Propp was also an amazing player in his youth. Playing for coach Gerry James, who had been a two-sport star with the NHL's Maple Leafs and Canadian Football League's Winnipeg Blue Bombers, Propp played 57 games with the Saskatchewan Junior Hockey League's Melville Millionaires in 1975–76. He scored 168 points. He joined the Brandon Wheat Kings of the Western Canada Hockey League and played 213 games in three seasons, tallying 511 points on 219 goals and 292 assists. Philadelphia drafted him 14th overall in 1979.

"Dunc McCallum, who coached me in Brandon, Gerry James in Melville, they helped along the way," said Propp. "Gerry had played in the NHL and he also played pro football at the same time! We didn't have drafts or anything like that. I had played with a Saskatchewan midget team the year before I went to Melville.

"Gerry wasn't just a good coach. He had a playbook, which I wish I still had. I attribute that to his football background. He had us skating with weight belts, lots of things that made us better. I don't think I was a mature person when I got to the NHL, but the things I learned along the way helped make me mature after I got there. The guys in the east are used to the big cities and the media attention. We're not used to that if we're from Saskatchewan, but because we're used to talking to people we can handle everything."

When Propp was growing up in Neudorf, he didn't play in the Weger Sports Complex. He predated that facility. "The old rink was near the highway," Propp said over the telephone from Philadelphia. "When I was there one summer, it must have been 1977, there was a 4H meeting going on. We were driving around on a windy day and I saw the rink sway and start to buckle.

"I had spent lots of time in that rink, often by sneaking in the chute where they shovelled the snow. We'd go there after school, but there were times reserved for public skating so we couldn't always get on the ice. With two brothers and one sister we would play a lot of street hockey, even under the lights with the neighbours, until our mothers would call us for supper. We didn't want to miss supper, so we'd go in, but we'd come back and play again sometimes.

"We always had a team in Neudorf because there was a group of six or seven guys, all about the same age. Sometimes we'd play with other age groups, but because we had a group about the same age we usually had a team for hockey, football, baseball, you name it. We'd travel together; I still know the highways around there."

Propp has followed Stoll's career, but he didn't know much about Litzenberger until they met a few years ago at a town reunion in Neudorf. Before he died in 2010, Litzenberger recounted the path he took to the NHL.

"It was a long way and a lot of hard work," said Litzenberger, "I grew up in Neudorf but we moved to Weyburn. I was always playing hockey. One day I came home and there were some fellows in my living room, sitting on the couch. They told me they wanted me to play for the (junior) Regina Pats. It was the best thing that ever happened to me because I got to play for Murray Armstrong, one of the finest men I met in my life."

Armstrong, a product of Regina, played in the NHL before returning home to coach the Pats in the 1950s. Litzenberger said his junior hockey coach was the person most responsible for an NHL career in which he won the Calder Memorial Trophy as the league's outstanding rookie in 1954–55 with the Blackhawks and, later, four Stanley Cups.

In the 1950s, many junior hockey teams were affiliated with NHL franchises — the Pats were part of the Montreal Canadiens' pipeline. Litzenberger initially joined the Canadiens, but he was gifted from one of the NHL's powerhouses to the struggling Blackhawks, and was their captain when they won the Stanley Cup in 1961. Traded to the Detroit Red Wings and then Toronto during the 1961–62 season, Litzenberger was with the Maple Leafs for Stanley Cup victories in 1962, 1963 and 1964. Subsequently sent to Toronto's American Hockey League franchise, he won Calder Cups in 1965 and 1966. A distant relative of Eddie Litzenberger's was at Stoll's Stanley Cup celebration in Neudorf.

"I'm a little closer to Brian Propp's age than I am to Eddie Litzenberger or Jarret Stoll," said Brian Litzenberger, who used to play senior hockey with Stoll's father. "Propp skated every day. We had an old rink uptown, but it blew down. Brian Propp would sneak into that rink every day to skate. He'd skate in the dark, right after school he'd go over there. That's the type of work ethic he had. Things like that stand out in a guy's mind. It didn't matter if somebody was there, you could sneak in almost anywhere. So Brian would sneak in with his brother, Greg, who's a little bit older. We sure followed Brian's career.

"When the Kings were on their Stanley Cup run and Jarret was playing, everybody followed it, but in springtime it's busy in a farming community. We would talk about it when you'd see each other after a rain. Everybody kind of roots for Jarret, but you give him distance. We talk about it because we all know what's going on, that kind of thing. A small community like this, we really appreciate that he always remembers us. He did a fund-raiser about six years ago and all the money from that helped our sporting facilities. We had a sportsman's dinner with Jarret, Eddie Litzenberger, Brian Propp, four girls who went to the Canadian championships. We had a dinner and an auction and stuff like that. It was the year Edmonton had gone to the Stanley Cup and didn't win it. Jarret was with the Oilers that year. It would have been kind of nice and we were hoping that Jarret would have had (the Stanley Cup) for that thing. It got us money for the curling rink and our minor ball system. He was here playing for a few years, and we found that little hockey jersey he wore for two or three years when he was here. We presented it to him today."

After spending the morning in Neudorf, Stoll and the Cup made the 50 mile journey northeast to Yorkton, where Sherri and Tim Stoll and their three children — Jarret, his older brother Kelly and younger sister Ashley — moved in 1992. Yorkton, a city of 15,000 people, held a parade in his honour. On the back of a red, antique fire truck, Stoll lifted the Stanley Cup over his head and smiled at the spectators taking his picture.

"Wasn't it awesome?" said Sherri Stoll. "It's so important to him: He's a small-town guy and he knows where his roots are. He was born and raised in Neudorf till he was 10, then we moved to Yorkton. Tim got transferred; he works for a grain company, which is why we moved to Yorkton. That's why (Jarret) brought it back to Neudorf and Yorkton, to show appreciation for everybody, not just the parents, the family, the coaches, his schoolteachers, just everybody."

Inside the lobby of Yorkton's Gallagher Centre, beside the hockey rink where the future NHLer played 14-and-under hockey and won a Western Canadian Bantam AAA championship with the Yorkton Terriers, Stoll posed again for about a thousand pictures. It took 2 1/2 hours for the entire lineup to pass through the lobby; the $10 per photograph was donated to Yorkton's KidSport, a charity that helps provide sporting goods and activities for children. Stoll apparently handled most of the day's costs, including the hiring of the Arkells, an up-and-coming Canadian band who really rocked when their host came on stage, Stanley Cup aloft, to sing a rendition of Bruce Springsteen's "Dancing in the Dark."

A fund-raising dinner attracted 1,100 patrons. In the autograph lineup were two cousins wearing Terriers jerseys, 16-year-old Tucker McMullen of Moosomin, Saskatchewan, and 18-year-old Devon McMullen, a member of the Saskatchewan Junior Hockey League's Terriers. Although the size of the lineup forced Stoll to rush lots of people through the photo sessions, the McMullen cousins were happy to get their picture taken with a local hero.

"He's a good two-way player, he's not a superstar, but he gets the job done for the team," said Devon McMullen. "He knows how to play the game. He's the type of guy you can look up to because he's a small-town guy. He never had as many options as some of the city kids. He used what he had."

At least four Kings fans from Los Angeles made the trip to Saskatchewan to pay homage to one of their favourite players. "We've been season-ticket holders 16 years now and we said if the Kings ever won the Cup we would travel to Canada to see the Cup because it's a Canadian sport," said John Hallman, nodding at his travelling partner from Los Angeles, Rob Mathieu. "We wanted to show that people in L.A. actually care about it and are passionate about it."

"His name might not be that well-known in L.A. but the real fans appreciate what Jarret Stoll has done for the team, they know him well," said Mathieu.

Added Hallman: "When he went from the second line to the third line, he didn't bitch about it at all. He just stepped up. Now he's known as the guy you want in the faceoff circle. He always wins the draw."

That's typical of a Saskatchewan hockey player — somebody you want on your team. He's the glue who holds the dressing room together. A back-checker. Somebody who never floats through a shift and doesn't care if his accomplishments are recognized by the fans or media, as long as his teammates respect his efforts. He remembers his roots, where he came from, who preceded him, who helped him, and he and respects the sport's tradition, how it binds Canada together on every frozen pond and indoor arena from Newfoundland to British Columbia.

The Saskatchewan players have a special bond, one they admittedly share with fellow NHLers from Western Canada. They remember freezing their feet and hands while skating on the outdoor rinks at every opportunity. They remember the parents, volunteers and friends who shovelled snow off the ice or flooded their backyards into miniature hockey rinks in the winter. They appreciate the coaches and teammates who gave them advice along the way, who helped them commit themselves to the game they love so they could play it at the highest level, keeping that passion in their hearts through every practice, game and commitment that goes along with being an NHL player.

Days after the Kings won the Stanley Cup, Stoll sent Barry Trapp a commemorative hat with a personal thank you. Trapp, a long-time scout with several NHL teams, who also served a stint as personnel director for Canada's junior hockey team, was asked to make a speech at Stoll's banquet in Yorkton. He brought along a Team Canada sweater for the occasion.

"I met Jarret through Hockey Canada, he was also on the under-18 team, two world junior teams, captain of the team in 2002," said Trapp, a product of Balcarres, Saskatchewan, midway between Regina and Yorkton. "I knew who he was when

I first saw him playing as a first-year bantam at the age of 14. When he really jumped out at me was when Saskatchewan won the under-17 championship; he was the captain. Through Hockey Canada we hit it off.

"With Hockey Canada you want to take the best players. One thing they said for sure is make sure you also take the best kids. There have been a lot of great kids, but this guy is the creme de la creme. There's something special from his upbringing. I watched Jarret today: He never changed his attitude, he never got tired of signing autographs or posing for pictures.

"When I was in Toronto, my first year (scouting) with Toronto, (Maple Leafs head coach/general manager) Pat Quinn said to me, 'Is there anybody out there you would like us to go after?' I said, 'Absolutely: Jarret Stoll. The guy's a winner, he's a leader, and you know what else, Pat, he can be the captain of an NHL team some-day, that's the kind of leadership he has.' So we made the deal, we made the trade. But Craig Button, GM of the Calgary Flames, was a minute and a half late sending it in to the NHL, so they cancelled the deal!"

"We kept in touch through emails over the years," Trapp continued. "I've followed his career. Once you put on this (Team Canada) sweater, you're family. You're with those guys for six weeks, only once or twice in a couple years, and you're family. You never lose that. Here's an example: I was (scouting for) Phoenix and we played Columbus. (Then-Columbus Blue Jackets forward) Rick Nash scored that goal where he went coast-to-coast. After the game I was outside the Phoenix dressing room and Rick was nearby getting interviewed by the Columbus press and everybody else. He said, 'Trapper! Gimme a minute, I'd like to talk to you.' I hadn't seen Rick since he played on the under-18 team, but that bond never breaks. You're family for life and you can never take that away from anybody. I'm getting goosebumps talking about it.

"The year we won it in '97, here's the Saskatchewan group: Mike Babcock coaching, Trent Whitfield from Alameda, Hugh Hamilton from Radisson, Peter Schaefer from Yellow Grass, Cory Sarich from Kenaston …You know why they're special: They're from small towns.

"There are no egos in Saskatchewan. Take Jarret Stoll, the captain of his team, plays on the power play, kills penalties. Comes to Hockey Canada — I say 'Are you willing to be a checker?' Without hesitation he answers 'Absolutely!' Whatever it takes, that's what Saskatchewan guys are like."

Ryan Getzlaf says there is a fraternity among
Saskatchewan players. It doesn't mater what the
age difference is, they know where they are from.

CAMARADERIE AMONG THE CURRENT CREW

Saskatchewan idolizes the Canadian Football League's Roughriders, whose annual souvenir sales exceed those of the other seven CFL franchises combined. Unfortunately, the province has never had an NHL franchise on which to lavish its loyalty. It nearly did. As recently as 2009, when a group named "Ice Edge" was trying to purchase the financially strapped Phoenix Coyotes, there were discussions about keeping the team in Arizona while playing up to five regular-season games in Saskatoon. Nothing came of the talk.

A more serious attempt to get a Saskatchewan-based team in the NHL came in 1983. The St. Louis Blues were virtually bankrupt and being dumped by their corporate owner, Ralston Purina. Bill Hunter, who had been the owner of the Alberta Oilers in 1972 when they became charter members of the short-lived World Hockey Association, attempted to purchase the Blues and move them to his home city of Saskatoon. Hunter, known as "Wild Bill" for his antics when he was involved with forming the Western Canada Junior Hockey League, easily got commitments from 18,000 potential season-ticket holders and obtained promises that an 18,000-seat arena would be built near

Saskatoon's downtown area. None of that impressed the NHL's governors. Instead, the league assumed ownership of the Blues before selling the franchise to Harry Ornest, who kept the team in St. Louis before re-selling it.

Despite the furor created across northern Saskatchewan about the possibility of luring the Blues — southern Saskatchewan basically pooh-poohed the idea of Saskatoon getting an NHL franchise — the province's hockey fans never developed much affection for the team from St. Louis. The roots of loyalty had been laid much earlier during the 1940s, '50s and '60s, when NHL teams sponsored junior teams across the country. The Regina Pats were sponsored by the Montreal Canadiens, which meant that many of the junior team's best players — such as Eddie Litzenberger, Bob Turner, Bill Hicke and Paul Masnick — became Montreal's property upon their junior graduation and thus created a strong alliance back home with the Canadiens. A similar allegiance happened with the Moose Jaw Canucks — whose top players like Fred Sasakamoose, the first Aboriginal player to play in the NHL, and Metro Prystai would advance to the Chicago Blackhawks. The Estevan Bruins and Weyburn Red Wings, long-time members of the Saskatchewan Junior Hockey League, also had sponsorship agreements with NHL teams, which are obvious from their nicknames.

When Hockey Night in Canada started televising games in 1952, weekly broadcasts almost always featured the Canadiens or Maple Leafs, so it was natural for Saskatchewanians to follow the fortunes of the two Canadian franchises. Anybody wanting to actually attend an NHL game, well, they had quite a winter's journey getting from Saskatchewan to Quebec or Ontario.

When the league expanded to twelve from six teams in 1967–68 season, the closest NHL team to Saskatchewan became the Minnesota North Stars, who played a mere 10-hour drive away from Saskatchewan's southern border with the United States. Certainly hockey fans felt an affinity for a team dealing with a similar climate and there were occasionally fan buses travelling from Regina to Minneapolis, sometimes with the advertised double feature of watching the North Stars on Saturday and the NFL's Minnesota Vikings on Sunday. But to say there was an onslaught of green North Stars jerseys throughout Saskatchewan wouldn't be true.

A rival upstart to the NHL, the World Hockey Association, began operations in 1972 and established pro hockey franchises in the two provinces bordering Saskatchewan. In Manitoba, the Winnipeg Jets won three WHA championships after enticing superstar Bobby Hull to leave the Chicago Blackhawks for an unheard-of-at-the-time contract worth $2.75 million over five years, and teaming him with Swedish stars Anders Hedberg and Ulf Nilsson. Two WHA franchises came to Alberta, the Calgary Cowboys and the Edmonton Oilers. The Cowboys, during their two-year existence from 1975 to 1977, had a smattering of Saskatchewan players on their roster but never built much of a following. The Oilers garnered more interest, particularly after acquiring a kid named Wayne Gretzky from the ruins of the Indianapolis Racers.

When the WHA ceased operations after the 1978–79 season, primarily because of financial woes, the four healthiest franchises — the Jets, Oilers, Quebec Nordiques and New England (renamed Hartford) Whalers — immediately joined the NHL.

Suddenly NHL teams were within a reasonable driving distance from Saskatchewan. The Jets, playing 325 kilometres from Saskatchewan's eastern border, were a fair-to-middling team with a few star players like Dale Hawerchuk and Paul MacLean, but they didn't exactly win over Saskatchewan's hockey fans. In Edmonton, 250 kilometres along the Yellowhead Highway from Saskatchewan's western border, the Oilers built a Stanley Cup-winning dynasty around Gretzky, Mark Messier, Glenn Anderson, Paul Coffey and Jari Kurri and acquired a strong fan base in Saskatchewan. In 1980, the arrival of the Flames in Calgary, 350 kilometres from the border, added another location for ardent fans from Saskatchewan to soak up the atmosphere of an NHL game.

Winnipeg had an NHL franchise from 1979 to 1996, when the Jets were sold and moved to Arizona as the Phoenix Coyotes. After the NHL assumed ownership of the Coyotes in 2009, speculation intensified that the franchise could return to Canada. Instead it was the floundering Atlanta Thrashers who were purchased by True North Sports & Entertainment, who re-located the team to Winnipeg and renamed it the Jets for the 2011–12 season.

Without an NHL team based in Saskatchewan, a reporter has to leave the province to track its best hockey players for face-to-face interviews. But walk into any NHL arena and head to the home team's dressing room, or the visiting team's dressing room and chances are there's at least one player in those rooms with Saskatchewan roots. During one nine-day, six-game stretch in December of 2011, such a parade of Saskatchewan players visited the MTS Centre, home of the Winnipeg Jets. Over the whole month, about a dozen of the 50-or-so Saskatchewan-born players on NHL rosters played in the Manitoba capital and, if you waited until the end of January, another dozen would have trooped through. During that December homestand of the Jets', only one visiting team — the New York Islanders — didn't have a Saskatchewan player in its lineup, a strange fact for a team that won four straight Stanley Cups in the 1980s with a roster that featured Saskatchewanians Bryan Trottier, Clark Gillies and Bob Bourne.

In the Jets' dressing room, only rugged forward Tanner Glass held a Saskatchewan pedigree. Glass was born in Regina, but spent his childhood in a couple of nearby towns, Craven and Southey, and attended school in Lumsden. He got in two fights during that six-game homestand. One was against former Pittsburgh Penguins forward Arron Asham.

As the punches subsided, Glass reached out and patted Asham on his left shoulder. Asham, after all, is nearly a neighbour, having grown up in Portage la Prairie, Manitoba, on the Trans-Canada Highway between Regina and Winnipeg

"That was a good fight," said Glass. "Since then, we've talk-ed about that one a couple of times. Arran Asham's from just down the road. He plays with the same mentality; all the Western Canada guys play with that mentality. It's like Wendel (Clark) or Selmar Odelein."

Odelein, a defenceman from Quill Lake who was a first-round draft pick by the Edmonton Oilers in 1984, had a promising hockey future derailed by knee injuries, but his younger brother Lyle Odelein parlayed his never-back-down style into a decent ca-reer with eight NHL teams, including the Cup-winning Montreal Canadiens in 1992–93. Clark, a forward from Kelvington, turned into a bona fide star with the Toronto Maple Leafs. Indeed, Clark's on-ice feistiness and off-ice demeanour made him a popular figure during his numerous NHL stops, idolized by legions of aspiring players throughout Saskatchewan. It seems like every player from Saskatchewan knows Wendel Clark, who maintains a high profile in the hockey world through his numerous public appearances, both paid and unpaid. Indeed, it seems like all the NHL players from Saskatchewan know each other in addition to crossing paths with stars from previous generations. Their camaraderie showed in their interviews, when I asked them what tied them all together.

"The Prairies in general produce a hearty group of people. You learn that you reap what you sow." said Kevin Cheveldayoff, who is in charge of hockey operations for the Jets. "I grew up on the farm; my father was a farmer, my mother was a school teacher in Blaine Lake (Saskatchewan). The two things they taught me, one, from my dad, is you have to have faith in what you do. When you put a seed into the ground, like he did, you have to have faith that it's going to grow into something. I learned from my mother, who's a schoolteacher, that you can never stop learning. Education is very, very important. Those are the two traits for me that are guiding lights. I think, in general, people from the Prairies appreciate hard work.

"We had the Blaine Lake Optimist Club, so I was very fortunate growing up because they sponsored everything, like ice time, which was very affordable for our families to play. We had very small teams, so sometimes we would be playing two or three different age levels at one time just to put teams together. Sometimes we would combine towns, for provincials, but we might go to tournaments and play one game at one level, another game at another level. We were just praying somebody didn't show up from another level so we could play at that level, too. We'd have a hamburger, a hot dog, and we'd be all set.

"We had natural ice. We had scrapers. It was a badge of honour for the parents to be scrapers. As kids we would watch the senior hockey teams then try to sneak out to be the scraper because we'd get a hot chocolate between periods for scraping the ice if we were fortunate enough.

"I didn't have to sneak into the rink. We had very dedicated people looking after the rink, a group of people, and it seemed like it was open all the time. Certainly it was open whenever we needed it. It was the fabric of the community. Dad was never a coach, but he had a pickup truck with a camper on the back where you would pile all the kids and go to all the games. That brings back great memories.

"From the small-town fraternity, there is a kinship or an association that's always going to be there, whether it's a loose association or a strong bond. Guys like Todd (McLellan, a Melville-born product and coach of the NHL's San Jose Sharks) and I played together in the Islanders' system. His brother and I played midget hockey together. There are lots and lots of players who over the course of time have gone on to prominent fields in the National Hockey League. It's not just people from Saskatchewan, but I don't think anyone forgets their roots.

"I moved from Blaine Lake to play with the (midget AAA Saskatoon) Blazers. To this day... you move away from home, you live with a family. You're fortunate those families take you into their home. That extends on to junior hockey. I was fortunate to come to Brandon, which was a great organization that kind of led me to here.

"There was no choice from my standpoint. I was recruited heavily by lots of colleges because my grades were good, but for me there was never a thought of not going major junior. I was very excited the day Brandon listed me; I was going to play major junior.

"The (Saskatoon) Blades organization was very strong, with great management, and I grew up around it, idolizing a lot of those players and playing with some of them coming up. When I was with the Blazers, guys like Wendel Clark were with the Blades. My head scout now, Marcel Comeau, was the Blades' head coach — we joke about that now. Bob Owen (an amateur scout from Regina) wanted to retire this year, but I talked him into working another season. Those associations run deep with guys like (Jets radio and TV play-by-play announcer) Dennis Beyak, who was with the Blades. We talk lots about those days moving forward. My very last question at the press conference when I was hired was, 'Riders or Bombers?' I'm like, 'You put me right on the spot, but one thing you're going to learn is I don't change my colours easily.' I was a Riders fan, but I enjoyed seeing the Bombers do well (reaching the Grey Cup in 2011)."

Anaheim Ducks captain and Regina native Ryan Getzlaf may have the highest-profile of the province's current crop of players, although there are numerous rivals for this honour: Some who come to mind are Regina's Jordan Eberle (Edmonton Oilers), Aneroid's Patrick Marleau (San Jose Sharks), Carlyle's Brenden Morrow (a long-time member of the Dallas Stars who was traded in 2013 to the Pittsburgh Penguins) and three players on the Philadelphia Flyers — brothers Luke and Brayden Schenn, from Saskatoon, and Regina-born Scott Hartnell.

Getzlaf played junior hockey with the WHL's Calgary Hitmen and was drafted 19th overall by Anaheim in 2003; his NHL career started in 2005. He signed a new, eight-year contract in 2013 worth $66 million. He regularly visits his family in Regina and spends his offseasons near Kelowna, British Columbia. The high-scoring centre acknowledges there is a fraternity among the Saskatchewan guys who, despite their disparate ages, seem to know each other, which part of the province they hail from, the divergent paths they took to the NHL and the teams for which they currently play.

"There's some of the guys I know, some I don't know, from across the province, being as small as it is," said Getzlaf, minutes after the Ducks lost their second game in two nights, 5–3 to the home-town Jets on the second game of a five-game road trip.

"I might not know them, but I know who they are. You definitely say 'Hi' to the other guys from Saskatchewan. A lot of the guys I grew up with, playing with them in Sask First, Team Canada, all that stuff. I also got to watch a lot of them when I was growing up. (The Saskatchewan Hockey Association) did a lot for me when I was growing up. I played summer hockey at a lot of different events. I played a lot of big games at a young age, with and against a lot of great players.

"I don't know if they're always the hardest workers because I've played with a lot of hard workers, but players from Saskatchewan play a certain way because of how we were brought up."

Montreal Canadiens forward Travis Moen is from Swift Current, a city of 15,000 along the Trans-Canada Highway about 200 kilometres west of Regina that, despite its diminutive size, supports a Western Hockey League franchise and provides services for the farms and oil wells on the surrounding plains. Swift Current is built in a valley, hilly enough to hold an annual Soap Box Derby every Father's Day, featuring handmade, non-motorized go-karts that reach speeds of 50 kilometres per hour.

"There are a few players, some of them I know, from Saskatchewan," said Moen. "Obviously the ones close to my place, like Patrick Marleau and (Maple Creek native) Zach Smith of Ottawa — we train together in the summer — are definitely guys you give a little nod to once in a while and talk to after the games. You definitely keep an eye on them. You want to see them do well. It's all about the families doing lots of hard work for you at an early age. We appreciate what they've done for us; we never had a lot of money but they drove us everywhere to play the game of hockey, the game we love. We owe a lot to our parents.

"Obviously the Roughriders are huge to everybody from Saskatchewan. I don't know what else it is that links us. There are lots of small-town guys from Saskatchewan, so it's pretty cool to come from small towns all the way to the NHL.

"They're more rugged, I think, farm boys or prairie boys. There are lots of skilled guys, too, but the typical knock on them is that they're more rugged, gritty, dump it in the corner, run you in the corners. That's somewhat my game, too."

Minnesota Wild backup goalie Josh Harding, forward Darroll

Powe and defenceman Nick Schultz, who was soon after traded to the Edmonton Oilers, are from Regina, Saskatoon and Strasbourg, respectively. They comprised a cross-section of Saskatchewan heritage on the Wild. Saskatoon is closer to the centre of Saskatchewan, a 2 1/2-hour drive northwest of Regina, placed on the scenic shores of the South Saskatchewan River. Saskatoon's citizens boast about having the bigger college campus, the University of Saskatchewan, and surpassing Regina about 20 years ago as the province's biggest city. According to a 2011 census, Saskatoon's population was 222,000 and Regina's was 193,000. Strasbourg is a farming community, about 45 minutes by car northwest of Regina, with a nine-hole golf course and, of course, an indoor, artificial-ice hockey arena and curling rink.

For that 2011–12 season, the Jets were playing in the NHL's Southeast Division, serving as last-minute replacements for their defunct predecessors, the Atlanta Thrashers. The NHL's plan was to move the Jets into the more geographically correct Central Division, but that got waylaid while the league concerned itself from September, 2012, to January, 2013, with getting a collective bargaining agreement in place that allowed the players and owners to evenly split all league-generated revenues. The NHL began its 48-game, 2013 season on January 19 with the Jets still in the Southeast Division, just like in 2011–12, when the Jets were regularly playing host to their divisional rivals: Washington Capitals, Florida Panthers, Tampa Bay Lightning and Carolina Hurricanes.

Washington forward Brooks Laich was repeatedly in Winnipeg, close enough for his family and friends to visit him from Wawota, a quaint town in Saskatchewan's southeast corner, in the middle of oilfields and grain fields, close to Moose Mountain Provincial Park. It's a town of 600 intent on keeping its school alive and its senior hockey team, the Flyers, competing in the Big Six Hockey League.

"Usually when I line up against a Saskatchewan guy I know where he's from and say, 'He's a good Kindersley boy' or something like that," said Laich, mentioning in particular Braydon Coburn, a member of the Philadelphia Flyers, and Derek Dorsett, a Columbus Blue Jackets draftee who was traded in 2013 to the New York Rangers. Coburn spent his childhood in Shaunavon, in the province's southwest corner, and Dorsett's from Kindersley, a couple hours to the north.

"You usually know where they're from and somewhere along the line, whether it's at an event or a hockey game or something through hockey, we've played against each other, met each other or know each other," continued Laich. "Golf tournaments, whatever it is. It's nice to see guys from home doing well."

None of the Saskatchewan players had an obligation to get interviewed inside the MTS Centre for the purposes of this book. Moen, Glass and Laich made their time available following pregame skates and they were more than willing to talk about anything Saskatchewan related. Harding, Powe and Schultz were on tighter schedules and hadn't been asked in advance if they could sit for a few minutes, so they weren't around when the Wild's game ended. Indeed, the Ducks had a hectic travel schedule so they didn't even conduct a traditional pregame skate. Setting up an interview with Getzlaf could have been difficult because NHL players are approachable by the media for a few minutes following a game, with the expectation that the questions will be game-oriented. But when a Ducks media director asked Getzlaf before the game if he would be willing to talk about Saskatchewan, the big power forward was agreeable. He graciously sat for one-on-one questioning about his upbringing while the assembled media, some on tight deadlines, waited for him to finish so they could ask questions about Anaheim's latest loss.

Pittsburgh Penguin forward Chris Kunitz had no such obligations. Kunitz was hobbled before the Penguins' game in Winnipeg, so he didn't participate in the team's pregame skate.

"He doesn't have to do any interviews if he's not skating," said a Penguins representative, who was asked if he could deliver this message to Kunitz:

"The questions will strictly be about Saskatchewan, from a Saskatchewan writer, with nothing about injuries or the team's performance."

"I'll check with him," said the Penguins rep, as he spotted Kunitz leaving the trainer's room. Twenty seconds later, Kunitz was reminiscing about growing up in Regina and practising in the small towns nearby.

"It seemed like we were always practising in Pense," Kunitz said about the town just west of Regina. "They had the best fries!"

Kunitz is one of 10 players who played in the NHL in 2013 whose birth certificate say they were born in Regina; 87 Regina-born players had appeared in the NHL's first 95 seasons, beginning in 1917. Kunitz, who was seventh in scoring in the NHL in 2012–13, has been away from Regina for a long time, but he was part of a Saskatchewan triumvirate as a teammate of Getzlaf and Moen in 2006–07, when the Ducks won their Stanley Cup.

"I've had the pleasure of playing with some Saskatchewan guys and against some Saskatchewan guys," said Kunitz. "With Getzlaf and Moen we've been able to keep in touch even though we're on different teams, in different conferences now.

"I think it's more of a Western Canada mentality that we have in common. I wasn't a guy who played in the WHL, but there's that style of being physical, skilled players with some intangibles. It's how you played the game growing up. If that's the way you watched it, that's the way you try to play."

Like players from other provinces, there are numerous paths

to be taken from small-town rinks to the luxurious arenas of the National Hockey League. Each player's journey is unique. Kunitz was enrolled in Hockey Regina's minor programs until Grade 11, when he moved away to Yorkton to play midget (16-and-under) AAA hockey. After a stint with the midget Yorkton Parkland Mallers he joined the Saskatchewan Junior Hockey League's Melville Millionaires for two seasons then enrolled at Ferris State University in Big Rapids, Michigan.

"There was never that (major junior opportunity)," said Kunitz. "I was a late bloomer. Maybe as a pro, too — one year in the minors, then the lockout (of NHL players that cancelled the 2004–05 season), then I kind of came to the NHL. It was one of those things. I took maybe the not-so-walked path to the NHL. I like the path I took, it definitely helped me in my career, helped me get a little stronger, helped me gain some confidence in my game.

"I've been gone since I was 16 or 17, so there's the maturity thing and the education thing. I had to pick up a couple (high school) classes to get my grade point average high enough to be able to get into college. You have families that take you in as billets, so still being friends and sharing things with those people is important. It's a big community across Saskatchewan. I still keep in touch with my billets, my parents stay in touch with them. They came down to our wedding in 2008. There's that great community of people in Saskatchewan who really love hockey."

When Kunitz was given his traditional day with the Stanley Cup following Anaheim's victory in the summer of 2007, he started his day in Big Rapids, Michigan. After sharing the Cup with his "college" family, a plane ride brought him and the trophy to Regina for a tour around Riffel High School, his alma mater, and a late night with his friends before passing the Stanley Cup to Getzlaf, who kept it in Regina, and then Moen, who took it to

Swift Current.

"I've always wanted to take (the Stanley Cup) back because those are the people who supported you," said Kunitz. "Being able to split that day, half at college, half at Riffel, it's a busy day, but you try to share it with people who mean the most: Minor-league coaches, old teammates, people who helped throughout your career, like the people who took you to tournaments when your parents couldn't go because your brothers had something else going on. It wasn't just immediate family. It was everybody you grew up with."

A budding superstar, Jordan Eberle
is already an alternate captain with
the Edmonton Oilers.

TWENTY-
SOMETHING

Saskatchewan has been producing NHLers since the 1920s, when a handful of players moved eastward to play pro hockey in the league that had been formed in 1917 with four franchises: Montreal Canadiens, Montreal Wanderers, Ottawa Senators and Toronto Hockey Club. An American team, the Boston Bruins, joined the loop in 1923 and the NHL became a six-team league in 1924. The makeup of the franchises kept changing until the "Original Six" held constant from 1942–67. In 1967–68, the Boston Bruins, Toronto Maple Leafs, Montreal Canadiens, Detroit Red Wings, Chicago Blackhawks and New York Rangers were joined by six expansion teams — St. Louis Blues, Los Angeles Kings, Philadelphia Flyers, Pittsburgh Penguins, Minnesota North Stars and California Seals. The league continued growing to the point where there are now 30 franchises — seven in Canada and 23 in the U.S. — and it has caused an increased demand for players. More and more players are joining the NHL from the U.S. and Europe, while Saskatchewan has also continued supplying the league with talent. Saskatchewan-born players accounted for 47 roster spots in April, 2013.

Way back in the NHL's early years, specifically the 1920s,

the pioneering group from Saskatchewan consisted of: Regina
Pats product Laudas "Duke" Dukowski, who played 200 games
between 1926–34 with the Chicago Blackhawks, New York
Rangers and New York Americans; Fort Qu'Appelle's Eddie
Shore, a future Hall of Famer who spent 13 1/2 seasons with
Boston before being traded to the New York Americans in 1940
and subsequently retiring to run the Springfield Indians American
Hockey League franchise; Saskatoon-born goalie Hec Fowler,
who played seven games with Boston in 1924–25 and was evi-
dently the first Saskatchewanian to play in the NHL; Fleming's
Fred Gordon, who played 38 games in 1926–27 with the Detroit
Cougars and 43 games in 1927–28 with Boston; Weyburn's
Gizzy Hart, whose final NHL season of five, in 1932–33 with the
Montreal Canadiens, came after spending five years in the minors;
Saskatoon's Lloyd Klein, who joined Boston as an 18-year-old in
1928; and Saskatoon's Earl Miller, who followed two seasons with
the University of Saskatchewan Huskies and two with the senior
Saskatoon Sheiks by beginning a seven-year NHL career in 1927.

That group started a proud tradition which continued through
subsequent generations with the likes of Murray Armstrong of
Regina, Sid Abel of Melville, Gordie Howe of Floral, Johnny
Bower of Prince Albert, Metro Prystai of Yorkton, Murray Balfour
of Regina, Dave Balon of Wakaw, Blair Chapman of Lloydminster,
Ron Greschner of Goodsoil, Brent Ashton of Saskatoon and Kelly
Buchberger of Langenburg, all former NHLers and among the
487 (as of April 1, 2013) Saskatchewan-born players who have
appeared in a regular-season game.

The tradition they fortified is still being honoured by talented, current, young players like Jordan Eberle (Regina) of the
Edmonton Oilers, Maple Leafs centre Tyler Bozak (Regina), brothers Luke and Brayden Schenn (Saskatoon) of the Flyers, Lightning
defenceman Keith Aulie (Rouleau) and dozens of others.

"I can probably name quite a few of them," said Eberle. "Every time you get a Saskatchewan kid on your team you get excited. First thing I looked at when we traded for Nick Schultz was, where's he from? Strasbourg! He's a Saskatchewan kid, so he must be a good guy. He's a great guy. Steve MacIntyre, who played with us when I joined the Oilers, is from near Kindersley (the village of Brock). The list goes on. You go back to your roots immediately.

"When you talk about Gordie Howe and Johnny Bower, that's a little before my era, and it's an incredible honour to think that I'm a part of that. My grandmother used to babysit Bryan Trottier, so our connection goes way back."

When the National Hockey League reconvened in January 2013, after a contract dispute convinced the owners to lock out their players for 113 days, Jordan Eberle was 22 years old. As property of the Edmonton Oilers, he had been dispatched during the lockout to play for their farm team, the Oklahoma City Barons of the American Hockey League, along with his younger teammates Taylor Hall and Ryan Nugent-Hopkins. When the lockout ended, the youthful trio of first-round draft choices rejoined the Oilers and occasionally found themselves playing together on the same forward line. Eberle was actually the old-timer, having been drafted 22nd overall in 2008 when, like most draft choices, he was 18. Hall was the first overall pick in the 2010 draft and Nugent-Hopkins was chosen first in 2011. Drafting first overall for an unprecedented third straight year, the Oilers chose Nail Yakupov with the initial selection in 2012, stockpiling their team with prospective superstars.

"You don't really know where hockey is going to take you," said Eberle. "You dream about (playing in the NHL) from a young age. I excelled with kids my own age and was always moving up in age groups. But you don't really know, you just dream and work towards it."

When they returned to Edmonton, Hall and Eberle shared an apartment during the NHL season. There are humourous video clips available on-line showing them trying to settle into household duties between time spent playing video games and, their most important task, attending practices and games as they worked toward bringing the Oilers back to respectability. When they spoke about their apartment's bleak decor, their lack of cooking skills, and that Eberle's mother Lisa provided them with most of their household necessities, it's a reminder of how young some players are when they get to the NHL. That's particularly true for the products of junior hockey such as Eberle, Hall (born in Calgary; junior team: Windsor Spitfires), Nugent-Hopkins (born in Burnaby, B.C.; junior team: Red Deer Rebels), and Yakupov (born in Russia; junior team: Sarnia Sting).

Eberle, who played junior for his home-town Regina Pats, was one of 27 Saskatchewan-born players who would still be in their 20s when the NHL's abbreviated 2013 season ended.

Twentysomething 20-somethings... Why so many?

"I get that question a lot: Why are there so many NHL players from Saskatchewan?" said Eberle. "It's coming up more because there are lots of younger guys in the NHL from Saskatchewan. We're obviously not the biggest province; look at Ontario and the number of players they support because of their bigger population. It's not just Saskatchewan, it's the West. It's something about that western persona — you're just an all-around good guy (laughs). They are all-around guys.

"Hockey's a team sport and these are guys who aren't just thinking about themselves. That goes a long way. Guys want players like that on their teams. Coaches recognize players like that. And some of the coaches come from Saskatchewan."

Eberle scored the biggest goal in the history of the world junior hockey championships, according to a poll conducted by TSN, when his forehand-to-backhand tally with 5.4 seconds remaining in the 2010 semifinal sent Canada's game against Russia into overtime. Eberle subsequently scored the shootout winner in a 6–5 decision, propelling Canada into the final and on to win the gold medal two days later with a 5–1 victory over Sweden.

Eberle is proud of the goal, moreso of the gold medal, and when he's repeatedly quizzed about it he always credits teammate Ryan Ellis for keeping the puck in the Russian zone and John Tavares for steering the puck in Eberle's direction.

Nine months after his monumental junior goal, Eberle scored his first NHL goal on the night the league opened its 2010–11 season. That debut goal instantly made the weekly highlight reels, leaving almost everyone slack-jawed with his toe-drag, forehand-to-backhand move that went into the Calgary Flames net. Where did he learn those moves, especially that lethal backhand?

"Haha," Eberle said in a text message via his cellphone. "Janzen Crescent is where I perfected it."

Street hockey games! Eberle grew up on Janzen Crescent in Regina, in an east-end suburb called Richmond Place, with his parents Lisa and Darren, sisters Whitney and Ashley and younger brother Dustin. There were about a dozen kids living on Janzen Crescent, often supplemented by the friends Eberle and his siblings would invite over for the shinny games that could start at any time. Just like the street-hockey scenes in Tim Hortons television commercials or the movie "Wayne's World," written by and starring Canadian Mike Myers, when the shinny games are interrupted by a passing vehicle someone yells "Car!" The nets are moved aside, the car passes, the nets are returned and the action resumes with a yell of "Game on!"

Eberle was born in 1990 and grew up as a phenomenal, high-scoring player in his minor hockey days, earning invitations from powerful, out-of-town travelling teams to join them for exclusive tournaments. He liked baseball, but his devotion to hockey convinced him to ditch all other sports so he could skate year-round, including the summers he spent travelling North America.

"I remember being at the Edmonton Brick tournament when I was 10 years old," said Eberle. "I was playing for the Vancouver Vipers; they had asked me to play for them. Travis Hamonic (now of the New York Islanders) was on the Vancouver team; on the Toronto team we played in the final: Steven Stamkos (Tampa Bay Lightning), Michael Del Zotto (New York Rangers), Alex Pietrangelo (St. Louis Blues). It's funny, you see them when you're 10 years old and still see them today. We beat them in overtime. I remind them about that."

Eberle actually scored that game-winning, overtime goal in the Brick tournament. So his penchant for big-time plays started a long time ago.

Eberle may be one of the NHL's brightest young stars, but he's going to need a few more stellar seasons to match the exploits of Regina-born Ryan Getzlaf, who turned 28 in May 2013, two months after signing an eight-year contract extension that averages $8.25 million US annually. Getzlaf, a Stanley Cup winner and captain of the Anaheim Mighty Ducks, joined the team in 2005 and averaged 0.94 points per game during his first 540 NHL contests. In Eberle's first 175 NHL games he was averaging 0.79 points per game and had just signed a six-year, $36-million deal.

Never mind the contracts and the scoring statistics. Just looking at the group of 20-somethings from Saskatchewan shows that the province is continuing to supply talented players to the NHL.

"In Toronto we had Tyler Bozak, Colby Armstrong, Luke Schenn — it's Western Canadian guys," said Aulie, a towering defenceman who was the WHL's Scholastic Player of the Year in 2007 when he played for the Brandon Wheat Kings.

Aulie got dealt from the Maple Leafs to Tampa Bay in 2012. Armstrong is a Lloydminster product who turned 30 before joining the Montreal Canadiens in 2013 for his ninth season with a fourth different NHL team.

"We kind of group up," said Aulie. "I guess we have a lot more things in common, things we can talk about. We've got common friends, everything else. There are so many guys from the Western league, if you don't know them you get to know them because you've heard of them before or you have common friends. It's that way and it makes things easier. We've got a lot in common. Some of the guys from Saskatchewan, we've even played high school sports against each other."

Bozak took a little longer to reach the NHL, arriving in Toronto as an undrafted free agent in 2009. Bozak had unsuccessful try-outs with WHL teams, so he played three seasons of Junior A hockey in British Columbia before enrolling at the University of Denver. A knee injury shortened his sophomore year, but he made the conference's all-academic team before being wooed by several NHL teams and signing with Toronto. Bozak was 26, a veteran of three seasons, when the Maple Leafs opened training camp in January 2013, where he ultimately earned a spot on Toronto's top forward line.

"I started in Regina and played here until after AAA (midget)," Bozak said during a summer visit at home with his parents Mitch and Karon and older brother Justin. "You always see (Hockey Regina) producing guys. Getzlaf and (Chris) Kunitz got there before me, but when you see guys advancing from the system you're in it gives you hope and it gives you motivation. I had great coaches all along, plus I was lucky enough to have my dad coaching me for lots of those years.

"I remember having lots of practices in Pense (a town just west of Regina), early in the morning. I even remember the odd practice in Gray (a village south of Regina); we had to shovel the ice because they didn't have a Zamboni. We really liked it and it was obviously a lot harder on our parents, having to get up. At that age we were just excited to get out there.

"I was lucky enough to have a rink in my backyard. Me and my brother helped my dad. In the first couple years we had a big tree right in the middle that we had to look out for. After that we cut it down. My dad cut it down; we were there to help but I don't think we really did much. We had that rink a long time — I remember our mom yelling at me and my brother all the time to get off and come in for supper. We wrecked the fence a few times by hitting it with pucks. Our mom and dad weren't too happy about that.

"We lived right beside the elementary school I went to (Ethel Milliken), directly beside it, so even at recess I would run home and try to sneak onto the ice. I'd get my skates on real quick and maybe get 10 minutes out of it. It's what makes you better. You're not doing drills or anything, you're just out there skating with the puck. It really helps in the long run. We got on the ice at a pretty young age and it was always competitive between me and my brother. We were always battling, trying to be better. I wanted to be on the ice more than him and he wanted to be out more than me. Then our dad would come out there; he could beat us every single time until we got a little older, then we started beating him. It was always the goal, to beat him, I think."

At that early stage it didn't really look like Bozak was destined for the NHL.

"I probably didn't start thinking I had a chance (at the NHL) until college," said Bozak. "During my last year of junior (128 points with BCHL's Victoria Grizzlies in 2006–07) I was able to lead the league in points and I got a lot of interest. It may have been in the back of my mind, but I was thinking about getting a scholarship. If something was to happen with hockey, great, but if not I had that education to fall back on. When I was younger I was always thinking NHL, playing with all the guys we'd call out who we were. I was always Pavel Bure. We would name every guy in the league back then.

"Some of the guys I play with bug us about being from Saskatchewan, about the farms and the country music. Maybe we listen to more country music than the other guys. Keith Aulie's from Rouleau — he's a farmer; his nickname was 'Big Rancher.' He must have been throwing hay bales around.

"There's not too much of that camaraderie on the ice, but you'll give the odd nod to the guys who are from here because you know them. For the guys I play with, we'll talk about the Roughies every now and again. Everybody from Saskatchewan cares about the (CFL's) Roughriders. I'm pretty sure Schenner, Army and I have had Rider gear on at some point."

Among the newest NHL prospects is Ryan Murray, a defence-man who was born in Regina, grew up in nearby Pilot Butte, played minor hockey in White City and played junior hockey for the WHL's Everett Silvertips. Murray was drafted second overall by the Columbus Blue Jackets in 2012. Murray remained with his junior team during the NHL's lockout, but in November he suffered a torn labrum in his left shoulder. The injury required surgery, forcing Murray to miss the 2012–13 world junior hockey championship, which is held annually during Christmas/New Year holidays, as well as the rest of his WHL season. It also delayed the opportunity to make his NHL debut.

"I was on skates at two, then I started playing hockey at four or five, probably five. When you're young you're just kind of play-ing and it's every kid's dream, obviously, to play in the NHL," Murray said during the summer following his draft. "I never thought it would happen, never thought I would get this close. I'm not there yet; I've still got a lot of work to do if I want to get there.

I had some great coaches, great teammates, who helped me along. I wouldn't be where I am today without them."

Murray may be the up-and-comer, but he's already familiar with the group he's joining.

"Everyone knows who the Saskatchewan guys are," said Murray. "I don't know if there's a common characteristic. Obviously there's lots of guys who play at a high level and it's great that Saskatchewan hockey produces the talent it does. Every player's different, so it's tough to describe them. I think it's a source of pride being from Saskatchewan. A lot of people in America don't know where Saskatchewan is. They might think it's just a bunch of farms; there's a pretty big stereotype from other places. When you go down to the States, the rinks there are pretty nice. There are a couple of rinks in Saskatchewan that aren't very nice. When you're growing up, sometimes you don't know what the rinks are like, what the boards are like, what the lights are like. Nothing's really perfect. I think that teaches you a lot, too. You learn to work with what you've got.

"There's been a ton of great players from Saskatchewan. The list goes on and on. I hope to be part of it, but I've got a lot of work to do still. I've got to make the league first, that's what I'm working on first."

Jaden Schwartz is one step ahead of Murray. Schwartz played seven games for the St. Louis Blues at the end of the 2011–12 season, scoring a game-winning, power-play goal on his first shot, and after starting the lockout-shortened campaign in the minors he rejoined St. Louis for 45 games as a regular during his sophomore season.

"Like every guy I have to earn a spot," said Schwartz. "I'm focusing on improving, getting bigger and stronger. But like I said, like every guy I've got to earn a spot."

Schwartz was born in Melfort. His family settled in Wilcox,

the home of Athol Murray College of Notre Dame, where he attended high school and played most of his hockey through to the Notre Dame Hounds of the Saskatchewan Junior Hockey League. After two years at Colorado College, having been drafted 14th overall by St. Louis, Schwartz joined the Blues and, in essence, the Saskatchewan contingent.

"You know who's from Saskatchewan," said Schwartz. "You can tell. It's a Saskatchewan thing. It's hard to explain, but you know who they are, guys like Getzlaf, (Pittsburgh Penguins forward Chris) Kunitz, or even (St. Louis defenceman) Barret Jackman, (an Alberta native) who played for the Regina Pats. Some of the guys who played at Notre Dame, like (former NHLers) Wendel Clark, Rod Brind'Amour. (Long-time Colorado Avalanche captain Joe) Sakic played in Saskatchewan (with the WHL's Swift Current Broncos). I look up to them. When you're young you don't really realize it, but as you grow up, you really do. Hopefully younger guys will feel that way about me someday."

Also in the fraternity are Eric Gryba, a product of Boston College who was born in Saskatoon in 1988, and made his NHL debut as a defenceman with the Ottawa Senators on February 16, 2013, and three days later recorded his first assist followed within a month by a goal against the Tampa Bay Lightning; Blake Comeau of Meadow Lake who spent five seasons with the New York Islanders before being waived, then joining the Calgary Flames, who traded him to Carolina at the 2013 deadline; and Derek Dorsett, a Kindersley product, who was drafted by Columbus in 2006. Weeks after breaking a collarbone in March 2013, Dorsett was part of a seven-player deal that sent him to the New York Rangers. Boyd Gordon, a durable product of Regina who began his career with the Washington Capitals, turned 30 after joining the Edmonton Oilers for the 2013–14 season.

Five of the 20-somethings are goaltenders, starting with Cam

Ward, who was born in Saskatoon and raised near Edmonton. Ward turned 29 early in the 2013 season, his eighth with the Carolina Hurricanes, the team he backstopped to winning the Stanley Cup as a rookie in 2006. Ward won the Conn Smythe Trophy as the playoffs' most outstanding player. Ward's backup in 2013 was Dan Ellis, a 32-year-old from Saskatoon who was with his fifth team in an eight-year career.

Josh Harding played junior hockey for his home-town Regina Pats before being drafted by the Minnesota Wild in 2002. Harding was diagnosed with multiple sclerosis in 2012, but thanks to medication he was able to continue as Minnesota's backup goalie and earned the Bill Masterton Memorial Trophy in 2013 for his perseverance, sportsmanship and dedication to hockey. Next on Minnesota's goalie depth chart was Darcy Kuemper, a 1990-born Saskatoon product who played junior for the Red Deer Rebels.

In 2011–12, only his second season with the Washington Capitals, goalie Braden Holtby led the team on an impressive playoff run while wearing on his mask the flags of two provinces, Alberta and Saskatchewan, to signify that he was born in the border city of Lloydminster.

Devan Dubnyk is also among the group of Saskatchewan-born goalies, but that's as far as it goes. Dubnyk played junior with the WHL's Kamloops Blazers and was named the league's Scholastic Player of the Year in 2004 — four years before Eberle earned the award as the player deemed best able to handle the responsibilities of schoolwork and playing junior hockey. Dubnyk hardly lived in Regina and is reluctant to accept any accolades for his birth certificate. He laughed when asked about his Saskatchewan heritage while visiting with Eberle, his teammate, during a golf tournament in Regina.

"It's a free entrance to the club, but I don't feel like I earned it. Not yet," said Dubnyk, who took over as Edmonton's starting goalie late in his third season, 2011–12.

"They put in a lot of groundwork; I can't jump into the club.

"I've lived everywhere pretty much. Born in Regina, moved to Newmarket, Ontario, to Winnipeg, to Vancouver, then to Calgary, all before I was 10. My dad worked for IBM; he was doing some good work, so he got promoted and transferred, promoted and transferred. He's from North Battleford; my grandparents are still in North Battleford, so I have Saskatchewan roots. Playing in Edmonton and being in Alberta you meet so many people from Saskatchewan. Both our equipment managers are from Saskatchewan. Whenever I need something from them, I'm a good Regina boy. Whenever we're not getting along, I'm from Calgary.

"The people in Saskatchewan, it's just like Canada but even moreso. You come here, people are extremely nice. They're hard-working. Everybody appreciates each other. Nothing's taken for granted. Everybody works hard. I think that's why you see so many great players from out here; it's the attitude and work ethic they're born and raised with. Being born with talent helps them, but it helps them get where they are. It's cool to come here and see that. You can feel it in Regina, how many people are here and Ebs seems to know every single one of them. It's cool. It's not a village or a small town, so it's cool to have that sense of community."

Well-travelled defenceman Brett Clark, a native of Wapella who turned 36 on December 23, 2012, was the oldest Saskatchewan player to appear in the NHL during 2013. Clark spent one season with the SJHL's Melville Millionaires, one with the University of Maine and one with the Canadian national team before being a sixth-round choice of the Montreal Canadiens in the 1996 draft. That started an odyssey that led him through parts of two seasons in the now-defunct International Hockey League and eight in the American Hockey League, plus lengthy stops with the Canadiens, Atlanta Thrashers, Colorado Avalanche and Tampa Bay Lightning.

Without an NHL contract after the lockout, having been released by Tampa Bay, Clark joined the Oklahoma City Barons before being signed as a veteran free agent by the Minnesota Wild.

"I know Ryan Murray; his dad grew up in our town," said Clark, who recalls Brent Murray babysitting him as a kid in Wapella, a southeastern town on the Trans-Canada Highway. "Ryan would be playing hockey and I'd be on the ice skating with him. It's a small world. It doesn't matter where you go, how old or young you are, everybody knows who's come from Saskatchewan."

Brooks Laich played minor hockey in his home town of Wawota before joining the Tisdale Trojans of the Saskatchewan Midget AAA Hockey League.

HOCKEY NIGHT
IN WAWOTA

Snow and blowing snow.

That's the ominous, almost-daily weather forecast during Saskatchewan's winter months. Winters usually start in October and stretch into April, with temperatures during the really cold nights of January and February capable of dropping to minus-45 degrees Celsius, with a windchill making it feel even colder. Snow and blowing snow often make travelling throughout the province unsafe.

A clear, dry highway is a rare blessing during the three-hour drive southeast from Regina to Wawota, where a Big Six Hockey League Game is being played on this Sunday evening in January. Virtually every town along Highway 48 has an indoor arena, often standing beside a curling rink — Vibank, Odessa, Montmartre, Glenavon, Windthorst, Kipling, Kennedy. And they're all different — Montmartre's old, wooden arena is memorable because one wall forms part of the boards that surround the playing area, so there's nothing for an on-ice official to grab when he's jumping away from a puck or nearby players; Vibank's rink is a few decades newer, but not new, all-metal with a low ceiling that surely explains why it gets so cold inside the building when there's a hockey game in progress. Lots of Saskatchewan's older arenas were built in the 1960s, some as projects to honour Canada's centennial in 1967. Those rinks are disappearing and, indeed, towns that are close to Regina, like Milestone and Southey, have built new facilities that sometimes attract big-city teams for practices and tournaments.

Some of the older arenas have artificial ice, some natural ice, but all were — or remain as — centre-pieces of their respective communities, places where the kids gather from the surrounding streets or the nearby farms to play hockey, the parents would flip hamburgers or sell fries at the concession stands and volunteers would pitch 50–50 tickets, coach the teams, operate the score-clock and re-surface the ice. Broomball, figure skating or ringette would sometimes occupy the small-town arenas, but hockey has always been the predominant sport for youngsters, teenagers and the adults who play senior hockey.

Wawota, a pretty town nestled in the heart of Saskatchewan's wheat and oil fields, has iced a senior hockey team for generations, usually with a roster full of graduates from its minor hockey system. There are still several senior leagues around the province. There's even a website dedicated to senior hockey inside Saskatchewan — Wickeddeadly.com, which recently tried gathering information on the various senior leagues and listed them: Qu'Appelle Valley, Big Six, Fishing Lake, Prairie, Highway, Triangle, Notekeu, Wild Goose, North Saskatchewan River, Saskatchewan Valley, White Mud, Beaver Lakes, Fort Carlton, Treaty Six and Wheatland.

At the intersection of Wawota's Main Street and Railway Avenue, right across from the Conexus Credit Union, stands an easel with a hand-written notice: "Big Six Hockey...Carnduff @ Wawota...Friday 8 p.m." Below it in the same hand-writing: "Redvers @ Wawota...Sunday 7 p.m." It's tough to read the sign at night, under the streetlights, but it would be easy to spot during the daylight hours, reminding the residents of a big hockey weekend for the local senior team. The sign doesn't say where the game is being played, but the easel stands within viewing distance of the town's indoor rink, the Wawota Community Centre.

Inside the Wawota Community Centre, collecting admissions and selling "Pot O' Gold" tickets, is Don Horvath. With his son Dean, Don Horvath co-manages the Wawota Flyers of the Big Six Hockey League. Don can tell you the Wawota Community Centre was built in 1971, had an ice-making plant constructed and artificial ice installed in 1977, that the team has been called the Flyers since 1959 and, before that, was known as the Bruins.

"Back a few years ago, every town along Highway 48 had a senior hockey team, now I believe it's only us and Vibank," said Don Horvath, a duly elected alderman of Wawota whose affiliation with hockey dates back several decades. "The key is minor hockey: If you have minor hockey you should produce enough players to have a senior team. But most of the towns don't have minor hockey programs.

"We have guys working the (oil) rigs on our senior team. Some of them are pretty good players and they come from different places. We never had the same roster for two nights in a row this season because the guys have to work, so they can't always make our games. We carry a 25-man roster. It's the nature of the beast. That's how you roll."

Dean Horvath is the scorekeeper/public address announcer and he also helps updating league statistics on the Big Six Hockey League's website. There were nine teams in the Big Six Hockey League during the 2011–12 season, eight teams in 2012–13.

According to the league's website, in 1959 a new, four-team league was established "when the old Soo Line Hockey League seemed to be dying." The new loop took its name from a Lethbridge-based brewery, which sponsored hockey leagues in Alberta and Manitoba, and "over the years just about every small town in southeast Saskatchewan has been in the Big Six at one time or another. The number of teams in the league has risen and fallen at times and reached as many as twelve at one point. The competition has been fast and furious over the years and many rivalries have been formed as a result."

As this book was being written, the Bienfait Coalers moved into the Big Six championship series against the winner of the other semifinal series, a best-of-five affair that was deadlocked 2–2 between the Arcola/Kisbey Combines and the Midale Mustangs. Bienfait, a charter member of the Big Six Hockey League, ultimately won its third straight championship by sweeping the best-of-seven final against Arcola/Kisbey, increasing the Coalers' total to 13 league championships. No Big Six Hockey League team has won more. Wawota has won six league titles.

"We've got 14 players from Wawota and this area," said Dean Horvath, before heading back to the announcer's booth. "We have a couple of guys who drive a hundred miles for every game. We tried getting players from Brandon (Manitoba's second-biggest city, about 150 kilometres straight east of Wawota). They won't come."

"We're in the middle of nowhere."

Saskatchewan's population base is shifting. Since 1971 more than half of the province's residents have been living in urban settings, which describes centres of 1,000-plus residents. Now only 30 per cent of Saskatchewanians are rural residents. Despite the shift and the noticeable decline in the population of the rural municipalities, most of the towns are growing — between the census taken in 2006 and the census taken in 2011, Wawota went from

522 to 561 residents, Montmartre from 413 to 476 and Vibank from 361 to 374. But the province is also booming because of its status as a producer of oil, grains and potash, a chemical used in fertilizer that helps grow food around the world.

At one stage during the Sunday night game in Wawota, Dean Horvath took a moment on behalf of the Flyers to thank the volunteers who worked in the concession stands and helped sell tickets. In his next announcement, following a Flyers goal, he also publicly welcomed a newspaper writer who was researching a story on NHL players from Saskatchewan. Polite applause greeted each announcement. Between periods virtually every spectator scurried for the warmth of the lobby; some visited their friends and neighbours while others bought coffee and a snack, or sneaked outside to smoke a cigarette. The players trooped into their respective dressing rooms, past the trophy cases that showcased local talent like Boyd Anderson, Don McPherson and Kelly Brookbank. Out on the ice, a Zamboni flooded the ice surface. A Seattle Thunderbirds logo was on the Zamboni, a reminder that the Western Hockey League team had chipped in to help purchase the $30,000 machine.

The Flyers started their season slowly in the Big Six Hockey League, but a feisty, 3–2 victory over the Redvers Rockets — played before 400 fans inside the 40-year-old Wawota Community Centre — was Wawota's fifth straight victory. That's pretty impressive considering Wawota's best player — Brooks Laich — is playing for the NHL's Washington Capitals.

There are reminders throughout the arena that Laich played his early hockey in Wawota, There are signed photographs of Laich inside the Community Centre's lobby. One big, framed photograph is of Canada's 2003 junior hockey team, featuring Laich, which placed second at the tournament in Halifax after losing the final game 3–2 to Russia. But the best reminder is the Zamboni and its Thunderbirds sticker. Knowing that Laich played junior hockey for the Thunderbirds, who do you think convinced the WHL team to help purchase the machine?

"Where I'm from, Wawota, hockey is what brings everybody together," Laich said, recalling his hometown roots before a Capitals game against the Winnipeg Jets.

"Your parents volunteer at the rink, everybody's at the rink. If you're a boy you play hockey, if you're a girl you either figure skate or play hockey. I remember talking to my parents about this: Our hometown has 600 people in it, but when the Flyers would play a hockey game there would be 900 people in the rink. It brings people from outside the town together. Your hockey rink is the pulse of your community."

Laich played minor hockey in his home town and progressed to the Tisdale Trojans of the Saskatchewan Midget AAA Hockey League before continuing his junior career with the Western Hockey League's Moose Jaw Warriors and — following a bad trade by the Warriors — Seattle Thunderbirds.

Boyhood friend Cameron Smolinski recalls Laich's rise from minor hockey player to junior hockey star:

"Brooks and I have been friends since we were little. We played hockey together. Don Horvath coached us when we were younger. Skills-wise there were other players like Brooks, but they didn't work as hard. He kept getting better until he had to leave town to keep playing. He played midget hockey in Tisdale, then we'd watch him play in Moose Jaw. They're probably kicking themselves for trading him from Moose Jaw to Seattle. He got 94 points his last year in Seattle! I went with his mom to see him play in Seattle — every time he touched the puck the crowd would go crazy. I thought that was something special, a guy I played minor hockey against and they loved him in Seattle. His whole junior team stopped in Wawota one day when they were going to Brandon. I got invited to supper at his parents' house and there were all these big guys eating there. It was great!"

For his part, Laich remembers there was local inspiration for his journey. "My next door neighbour, Kris Porter, played for the (junior) Weyburn Red Wings," he said. "We used to go to Weyburn to watch him play. They had a superstar line, 100-point scorers, and he got a full scholarship to Merrimack College, a full ride. I remember looking at him and thinking, 'Holy cow! He plays for Weyburn!' We didn't have an NHL team nearby, so my next-door neighbour's playing for Weyburn, I knew him and he was sort of the first guy from our town to make it out of town to play. He didn't make the NHL but he played in the East Coast league. When I was a kid I had somebody right next door who had made it somewhere to play hockey. I thought it was the coolest thing and I realized I just had to keep working. What else would you rather do?"

Brooks Laich made it to the NHL despite being a late-round draft choice. He was selected in the fifth-round, 193rd overall, by the Ottawa Senators in 2001. He played only one game with Ottawa (on Feb. 3, 2004) before being dealt, with a draft choice, to Washington for high-scoring forward Peter Bondra — another lopsided trade that worked out well for Laich and his new team. Bondra played just 23 games with Ottawa. Heading into the lock-out-shortened 2012–13 season, Laich, a hard-working, two-way forward, had played 556 regular-season games for Washington. He was coming off a season in which he played all 82 games, had 41 points and led all NHL forwards with 92 blocked shots. He kills penalties, sees power-play time, occasionally serves as a linemate for Capitals superstar Alexander Ovechkin, is an alternate captain and recently signed a six-year contract extension worth $27 million. Laich was also the Capitals' player representative during the lockout that shortened the 2012–13 season, staunchly standing behind the NHL Players' Association and its leadership. Evidently popular with his teammates, he's also popular with the media, a go-to guy who is candid, honest and refreshingly quotable.

Laich is a bona fide NHLer, not at the superstar level of Ovechkin, Sidney Crosby, Rick Nash or Pavel Datsyuk, yet mentioning his name conjures up an immediate reaction. "Isn't Brooks Laich the guy who changed that flat tire?"

Yes, yes he is. After the Capitals, who had posted the regular-season's best record, were eliminated in the 2010 NHL playoffs by a seventh-game loss against the visiting Montreal Canadiens, Laich was driving his car across a Washington bridge when he spotted a parked vehicle with a flat tire. The vehicle's occupants were two female Capitals fans. Laich stopped, changed the tire and reportedly apologized to the fans for his team's loss.

"It's not a big deal," said Laich. "It was just a tire. A lady and her daughter were stranded on the side of the road. I figured my tire expertise outweighed theirs."

We're not saying a pro basketball player from the Washington Wizards, a member of the NFL's Washington Redskins or a hockey player from Alberta, Ontario, the Maritimes, Europe or the U.S. wouldn't have stopped to change that tire, but in Saskatchewan it's expected: Helping your neighbour, never forgetting where you're from. Which explains why Laich returns to Saskatchewan every offseason. He visits friends and family, attends charitable events and works extraordinarily hard at staying in shape, renting ice time during the summer with other pro players to attend power-skating sessions with Liane Davis, an instructor in Regina.

He even rallies other pro hockey players to the cause.

"I try to get these guys to stay in Saskatchewan," said Laich. "I give them a hard time. They always say they're Saskatchewan guys, so I say, 'Stay in Saskatchewan.' Our (offseason) skates are dwindling. Boyd Gordon, Jeremy Williams, they've moved away. Guys get married here or there and move away, so they come back to visit in the summer but they're not always there, so it hurts our skates. But there's some good, young players coming up: Brayden McNabb in Buffalo is going to be a stud of a defenceman, Jordan Eberle (Edmonton Oilers), I always thought Riley Holzapfel (an Atlanta Thrashers second-round draft pick in 2006) was a good player, Jaden Schwartz (St. Louis Blues) is a good kid. So many good, young players from Saskatchewan. Colby Armstrong (Montreal Canadiens) — I've never met him, but everybody I talk to says he's unreal. If I get on them early enough maybe they'll build a house there and skate with us. They're unselfish guys, good teammates, they've learned to be good teammates. A lot of times they end up being the sort-of glue guy on the team. I hope I'm like that. I really enjoy the guys I play with and I hope they enjoy playing with me. I've learned from some other good guys, like (former NHLers) Jamie Heward and Mike Sillinger."

Saskatchewan doesn't just produce hockey players — Buffalo Sabres general manager Darcy Regier is from Swift Current, San Jose Sharks head coach Todd McLellan was born in Melville, Phoenix Coyotes head coach Dave Tippett is from Moosomin and, although their birth certificates claim they were born outside the province, head coaches Mike Babcock of the Detroit Red Wings and Glen Gulutzan, who was dumped after the 2013 season by the Dallas Stars, spent formative years inside the province and are considered Saskatchewan products.

According to the Saskatchewan Hockey Association there are approximately 30,000 registered players ranging from senior to beginners, a number that has held fairly constant for the past decade or so despite the dwindling populations in rural communities. Counting officials, coaches and registered volunteers that number of registered SHA members swells to 40,000 and doesn't include many of the groups who get together for pick-up games at the outdoor rinks or the regulars who book the indoor rinks for a recreational, call-your-own-penalties scrimmage.

Saskatchewan has five franchises in the Western Hockey League and a 12-team Saskatchewan Junior Hockey League, whose champions are regularly challenging for national junior A crowns. The 12-team Saskatchewan Midget AAA Hockey League had produced five of the last seven national champions. There's also a provincial midget AAA league to highlight a flourishing women's program and two major universities with men's and women's programs. Remember that Hayley Wickenheiser, considered the best female hockey player in the world, hails from Shaunavon, a town in southwestern Saskatchewan.

To get around the rural to urban population shift, SHA officials note that smaller towns are simply combining their players to ice squads for competitions against the city teams from Saskatoon, Regina, Moose Jaw, Prince Albert, North Battleford, Yorkton, Weyburn, Estevan and Swift Current. It requires a lot of driving, often in winter conditions, to get to games throughout the province.

"At a very young age Saskatchewan players are hardened: You drive long hours through the winter to get to rinks," said Laich, "I drove 70 miles one way, three times a week when I was 15, from Wawota to Esterhazy, to play better hockey. My parents drove because I wasn't old enough to drive. You're hardened at a younger age. You're used to the elements. I don't know what it is, other than Saskatchewan-born players really have an appreciation for the game. They really love to play hockey, whether they're getting paid for it or not, they're truly fans of the game. That alone can carry you a long, long way."

Saskatchewan's communities proudly, publicly honour their hockey heroes. A sign outside of Aneroid pays tribute to Patrick Marleau of the San Jose Sharks. Two signs facing the Trans-Canada Highway at Wapella proclaim it the home of retired NHLer Dave Dunn and much-travelled NHL defenceman Brett Clark. Kelvington, a town of 1,000 residents that dubs itself "The Hockey Factory," might have Saskatchewan's biggest sign — it honours six former pro hockey players who have a connection to Kelvington, having been born there or nearby or having played there: Barry Melrose, brothers Wendel Clark and Kerry Clark, cousins Joey Kocur and Kory Kocur, and Lloyd Gronsdahl.

A prominent sign on the outskirts proclaims Wawota as Laich's hometown. The sign was constructed by the same guy who made Laich's weight-training bench when he was a kid; it was unveiled on Brooks Laich Day, an event held in the summer of 2009 that included a breakfast, golf tournament and a fund-raising supper. It was a way of the community honouring their hero and Laich thanking the community — something that comes natural to the NHLer and his hometown:

"I might have been Brooks' first hockey coach, me and his dad, Harold," said Don Horvath. "It was six-and-under hockey. We were teaching Brooks where to stand for faceoffs. A few years later he needed a sponsor so he could go to a tournament in Calgary, so my company sponsored him. When he made the Canadian junior team he sent a picture of the team to thank me. He signed it 'To Mr. Horvath.'

"We're all hoping Brooks stays with the Capitals. There are lots of Caps fans here, plus we would have to change the sign on the boards."

Indeed, an advertisement on the rink's boards, right beside the Wawota & District Lions Club, in Washington-uniform-red-and-blue reads:

Proud Supporters of Hockey in Wawota

The Laich Family

(Caps Fans)

Brooks Laich notices the adulation, but doesn't forget where he comes from. "I've got so many friends calling. My parents' phone rings every time I play. It keeps you humble. One of my friends called me after a game to tell me he saw me play — 'I'm so proud of you, you're in the NHL and that's the coolest thing ever, but I'm so glad New Jersey won tonight.' He's a huge Martin Brodeur fan, a huge New Jersey Devils fan. Cameron Skulmoski is his name. He collects hockey cards. He's got my world junior card, he collects all that stuff."

Skulmoski adds to the story: "When Brooks was with the Thunderbirds they helped raise money to buy the rink's Zamboni. Now we go watch Brooks play when he's in Edmonton or Calgary, whenever he's close by. There's usually so many of us there to see Brooks that they have to cordon off a little section for us."

"He knows I'm a fan of Martin Brodeur and sometimes he rubs that into me. If he plays against New Jersey he'll send me a text telling me that he scored a couple of nice ones on Martin, so I race to YouTube to watch the highlights. But here's the type of guy he is: He gave me a signed, game-used stick from Martin Brodeur. I told Brooks, 'I can't give you anything that will mean as much to you as this means to me.'"

When you drive around Wawota you have to notice the fire

hydrants, painted brightly as people or cartoon figures. On the outskirts of Wawota is a marsh; when it's frozen over, some local aficionados haul nets onto the huge ice surface for the makeshift hockey games played there. The town doesn't have a hospital, but it has a long-term care home, a health centre visited regularly by doctors, a bank and a credit union, one motel, a funeral chapel, a beauty salon and a pedicurist, a couple of gas stations, numerous businesses that cater to agriculture and oil companies, some baseball diamonds and a curling rink, which is just up the hill from the arena. South of the baseball diamonds is an airport, which is basically a field that can be used as a runway for small planes. There's also a K-12 grade school. Wawota is a 1/2-hour drive from Moose Mountain Provincial Park and White Bear First Nation; each features a lake for boating and fishing and can boast about maintaining a tremendous 18-hole golf course. The park contains a huge waterslide; the reservation has a casino. There's no shortage of things to do.

"When we were 13, 15 years old, we always had things going on, whether it was ball in the summer or hockey in the winter," said Cameron Skumolski. "If we had a day off school, the phones would be ringing and we'd be getting together to do things. If it was winter we'd go to the rink to play hockey. Sometimes we'd play all Saturday, until we could barely skate anymore. If the rink was busy we'd play out on the streets."

Laich's initials are probably carved somewhere into the structure of the Wawota Community Centre, considering how much time he spent in the building.

"I don't know if my parents know this," said Laich. "But I borrowed a key to the rink from my friend's dad. I went right away and got a copy of it made. So when I was 14, playing Sask First, I had a key to the rink and I would go over to the rink in the morning before school. The ice would have been flooded at night, so the next day the caretaker would show up and the ice would be chewed up. 'What's going on?' There was nothing else to do in town in the winter but play hockey. It was a way of life."

The caretaker didn't mind.

"We kind of knew there were a couple of keys out there," said Gordon Murray, who looked after Wawota's arena for many years with his wife, Sandra. "There would be two or three kids out playing hockey all the time, but nobody was here more than Brooks."

There are some hockey players who need no introduction to any generation.
Gordie Howe is one of those players.

A WESTERN HEART IN THE CITY OF BROTHERLY LOVE

The Philadelphia Flyers were outworking, outscoring and outplaying the Winnipeg Jets, justifiably leading their hosts 1–0 during an NHL game on April 6, 2013. About midway through the second period, Jets defenceman Tobias Enstrom blasted a rising slapshot from the blueline toward the Flyers net. Luke Schenn, a Flyers defenceman, started dropping down to block the shot before realizing it was flying at his head. Schenn fortunately turned slightly and, perhaps softened slightly by the visor attached to his helmet, absorbed the shot on the side of his face, just beside his right eye.

Schenn fell momentarily to the ice, play was stopped and, as blood streamed onto the ice and television commentators yelled that he had been hit in the face, Schenn shook off his hockey gloves and put his hands to his head as he skated quickly toward the gate leading to the Flyers' dressing room inside the MTS Centre. The Flyers' trainer was in hot pursuit.

Seven minutes later in the second period, Schenn returned to the ice, his gash stitched in two layers — six stitches internally and six stitches externally, he would tell his father. Winnipeg now led 2–1 on goals scored 27 seconds apart while Schenn was getting sewn together. During Schenn's first shift back on the ice, Evander Kane scored for Winnipeg. Before the second period ended, Bryan Little put the Jets ahead 4–1, the score that stood until the end of the game. From an observer's point of view: Losing Schenn, even temporarily, was the turning point of the game.

"He's one of the guys, top two or most hits in the NHL. You can really tell when he's on the ice. He's physical. He's blocking shots. Tonight he's sacrificing his head to block a shot," said one of Schenn's teammates, Scott Hartnell, another guy whose birth certificate shows his Saskatchewan roots. "That's the kind of stuff we need to build on, not cave after that."

Schenn's injury evidently turned the game in Winnipeg's favour and sent the Flyers to a crushing defeat while they were trying to earn a berth in the NHL playoffs, a goal they didn't attain when the 2013 season ended. Hartnell, one of Philadelphia's feistier players, was poking Jets players with his stick and taunting them, trying to get something sparked before the game ended. It was too late. After Schenn's short but destabilizing absence the Flyers couldn't re-group.

Schenn was self-effacing afterwards, answering the media's questions while wearing a backwards ball cap emblazoned with a Flyers logo, some blood still leaking from his wound.

"Usually a good D-man will get his head up," Schenn said with a smirk. "Sometimes they shoot high. He wound up, I just tried to get in front and block the shot. I was lucky. It could have been a lot worse."

Schenn's value to the Flyers is noteworthy because he wasn't a long-term veteran, nor someone whom the team had been assembled around. Schenn was instead a recent acquisition, having been traded to Philadelphia from the Toronto Maple Leafs just eight months earlier. Toronto received a gifted sniper, James Van Riemsdyk, but parted with a heart-and-soul defenceman, a physical presence who clears the slot, can conduct power plays, logs a lot of ice time and can deliver a crunching body check. He's a Saskatchewan guy who was thrilled about joining the Flyers so he could play with his younger brother, Brayden Schenn, a former first-round draft choice who had been traded to Philadelphia from the Los Angeles Kings exactly one year before Luke. Coincidentally, Luke had been the fifth overall choice in the 2008 draft and Brayden was taken fifth overall in 2009. They look enough alike to be brothers, but at 6-foot-2 and 229-pound Luke is obviously the big brother to 6-foot-1, 190-pound Brayden.

"The boys are best friends," Jeff Schenn, their father, said during a phone conversation from the family's home in Saskatoon. "They're inseparable. It's a great thing, it really helps them when they're having a tough time. It's nice to have that. I know they talked pretty much every night when they weren't on the same team. But to have each other, to go to the rink, to talk about different things and share this experience together, it's pretty cool! Philly's been great to Brayden and Luke. It's all worked out great."

Philadelphia's famous nickname — the "City of Brotherly Love" — derives from Greek words denoting a place where people of every colour, nationality, religion and upbringing can live in harmony. That may be the case, but it still feels fitting the City of

Brotherly Love has one of the very few same-team brother acts currently playing in the NHL. The Pennsylvania city is a long way from Saskatoon — 3,325 kilometres, 32 hours by bus — and has a population of 1.5 million, six times that of Saskatoon — but it is no coincidence that this particular brother act hails from Saskatchewan's largest city.

"I was talking to (Flyers general manager) Paul Holmgren," said Jeff Schenn, aware that Holmgren, an American, joined the Flyers as a player in 1976 and has also served the team as an assistant coach, head coach, scout, director of player personnel and assistant general manager. "He told me the Flyers used to go out and scout in Saskatchewan. Nobody used to do that in the early days; they used to go to the east lots, but the Flyers used to love to come out to Saskatchewan. I know they love those Western Hockey League guys."

The Flyers joined the NHL in 1967–68, when the league expanded to 12 from six teams.

Before that first expansion all "Original Six" franchises were located in Eastern Canada and the U.S., stretching south to New York and west to Chicago. As the league kept expanding, the demand for talent also grow accordingly, so teams hired scouts who grew up and lived in Western Canada, former players who had toiled in the minors and graduated to the NHL: Gerry "Tex" Ehman with the St. Louis Blues and ultimately the New York Islanders, Lorne Davis with the St. Louis Blues and later the Edmonton Oilers, Lou Jankowski with the New York Rangers and Gerry Melnyk with the Flyers.

Melnyk, a product of Edmonton, was the driving force behind

drafting Manitoba teenager Bobby Clarke, who became the captain and inspirational leader of the Flyers team that won successive Stanley Cups in 1974 and 1975. Clarke had led his home town Flin Flon Bombers to two league championships, plus a Canadian championship in 1969, topped the league in scoring two straight years and won an MVP award. Despite this impressive pedigree, Melnyk had to convince the Flyers that Clarke's diabetes would not slow him down at the NHL level.

Captained by the hard-working Clarke, the Flyers became the first expansion team to win a Stanley Cup and quite possibly the last NHL team to win the championship with a roster composed entirely of Canadians. The 24-man, all-Canadian roster that won the Cup in 1973–74 had 12 players from Western Canada, including four from Saskatchewan: defenceman Ed Van Impe from Saskatoon and forwards Dave "The Hammer" Schultz from Waldheim, Don Saleski of Moose Jaw and Ross Lonsberry of Watson. Schultz and Saleski were two of numerous fighters, Schultz perhaps the best of the bunch, on a squad dubbed the "Broad Street Bullies" for the take-no-prisoners approach taught by Flyers head coach Fred Shero. Philadelphia appeared in Stanley Cup finals again in 1976, 1980, 1985, 1987, 1997 and 2010, but hasn't won a title since its back-to-back championships. Clark has remained with the franchise for most of those years, primarily as general manager although he's now a senior vice-president overseeing the development of the Flyers' young players.

Philadelphia's long-established tradition of having a core of Western Canadians on its roster continues currently with the Schenns, of Saskatoon, Regina-born Scott Hartnell and veteran defenceman Braydon Coburn all having strong Saskatchewan connections.

Coburn was born in Calgary, but he grew up in Shaunavon, a hockey-mad town in the southwest corner of Saskatchewan that also produced Hayley Wickenheiser, long-time captain of the Canadian women's hockey team, and former NHL defenceman Rhett Warrener. Coburn had a stellar career with the Portland Winterhawks, which included winning the Doug Wickenheiser Memorial Trophy as the WHL player who shows the most commitment to his community. (Wickenheiser, a Regina product and a cousin of Hayley, had led his home-town Pats to a WHL championship in 1980 and was subsequently the first player drafted that year, by the Montreal Canadiens. Wickhenheiser played professionally until 1994 with five different NHL teams; he died of cancer in 1999.) Coburn was the eighth overall selection by the Atlanta Thrashers in the 2003 draft. Like Doug Wickenheiser, Coburn and his "Saskatchewan" compatriots are popular teammates, appreciated for their personalities off the ice and their work ethic on the ice.

"All those guys have a gritty side to their game," said Frank Seravalli, the Flyers newspaper beat writer for the Philadelphia Daily News. "The Schenn brothers really like to hit and Hartnell's made a living in front of the net — 16 power-play goals last year, second in the league, are a testament to his ability in front of the net. Hartnell has become a fan favourite. He has endeared himself to the fans; social media has really helped him introduce everybody to his sense of humour. Any opportunity he's had, he creates a spotlight and takes advantage of that. Being at the all-star game last year in Ottawa, he's the guy who picked up a BlackBerry and skated around with it. He's not afraid to be mic'd up during games. Hartnell can be a go-to guy (for media interviews). The Schenns, we're just getting to know them. Coburn's a thoughtful player, really thinks the game. Coburn is also the Flyers' most physically fit player. He spends lots of time outdoors when he goes home. His father has a ranch, I believe, in Saskatchewan, way up north. During the lockout he did a lot of snowmobiling and it was so cold that he needed to have a device to keep his visors heated up. He spends quite a bit of time outdoors.

"They're all pretty forthcoming and the one thing you can say about all of them is: They're honest."

Hartnell has a birth certificate claiming he was born in Regina, but he didn't live in the Queen City for any substantial time. Hartnell lived in Eston, Saskatchewan, for eight years before moving to "the Alberta side" of Lloydminster.

"I'd say I'm an Alberta guy, but we have roots everywhere," said Hartnell. "Most of my mom's family lives mostly in Saskatchewan. I played for Team Alberta in the Canada Winter Games, we won a national title in 1999, so I'd be an Alberta guy. We produce players the same way: In Alberta and Saskatchewan there's not much else to do in the winter time. It's such a long, harsh winter, but you bundle up, get the outdoor draft at school, play road hockey, play pond hockey.

"(With the Flyers) you're friends with everybody on the team, especially with the guys from out west, the guys who grew up on the Prairies, the guys who grew up on the farm. There's something instilled in us, part of our beliefs: If you work hard you get rewarded, you love your family, you stick together, all that kind of stuff. Everybody from Western Canada, whether they play for the Maple Leafs or all over the States, they're level-headed no matter what happens, even if you're making $1.20 an acre (as a farmer selling wheat)."

After playing junior A with his "hometown" Lloydminster Blazers, Hartnell joined the WHL's Prince Albert Raiders. A hard-driving power forward, in his last season Hartnell became Prince Albert's captain, led the team with 82 points, was chosen its most valuable player and got drafted sixth overall by the Nashville Predators in 2000. After six seasons with Nashville, and spending the 2004–05 lockout playing in Norway, Hartnell was dealt to Philadelphia, With his long red hair flowing from under his helmet, Hartnell is a flamboyant player who plays at full speed offensively and defensively and earns extra attention for his antics and some spectacular on-ice falls. He also gets out in the community for numerous fund-raising events during the season, which is part of his upbringing.

"It's one community, especially in Saskatchewan," said Hartnell. "It's not a big metropolis, it's somewhere where everybody's close, like family. It's always like that. I went back (to Eston) last summer and it was like I hadn't left in 20 years. It had the small-town feel to it, that once you're part of the community you're part of it forever. You remember growing up, it's the best time of your life, and you keep playing hockey."

When asked if they have a Saskatchewan clique on the team, with Hartnell, the Schenn brothers and Coyburn, all of them demurred and insisted that everybody on the Flyers is a part of the family. But there are certain groups that are tighter-knit. It's a lot like Canadian Football League teams, who aren't really divided within their locker rooms, but it's usually easy to see that the black players from the southern States tend to hang out together and usually end up as roommates, much like the white, Canadian kids from Eastern Canada, or the California dudes, or the offensive linemen. That's what happens when there's something — a philosophy, an upbringing, a language, a certain knowledge — that you share with someone else.

For the Schenn brothers, the road to Philadelphia began on Hurley Crescent in north-central Saskatoon. They were seldom on the same team within the Saskatoon Minor Hockey Association but they spent countless hours playing hockey with and against each other in their neighbourhood.

"On my street alone, it's funny, I would say on our short little block of Hurley Crescent there were five or six backyard rinks," said Luke Schenn. "And I betcha, just on that block alone, that 10 to 12 guys played in the Western Hockey League. I don't think it happened by fluke. We grew up playing backyard hockey every single day, street hockey in the summer and backyard hockey or pond hockey in the winter.

"Some days the other guys weren't around, if their families were going somewhere for games or education or they had other things to do. We weren't all the same age so we weren't all on the same team, but if everyone wasn't around it would be me and Brayden one-on-one in the backyard. I think that's how it kind of worked out, with him being the younger brother I would give him the puck, he's on offence and I'd be on defence. That happened a lot — I'm a defenceman and he's a forward. We played a lot of one-on-one that way."

Brayden Schenn played most of his junior career with the Wheat Kings from Brandon, Manitoba. The longest bus trip in the Western Hockey League is 2,150 kilometres, about 21 hours if travelled non-stop, from Brandon to Portland, Oregon, home of the Winterhawks. On such a road trip, Brayden's Wheat Kings would stop en route, usually to play games and stay overnight in Seattle, Spokane, Vancouver or Kelowna, B.C., where Luke toiled for the WHL's Rockets. The brothers' WHL careers overlapped for just one season, 2007–08, which was Brayden's first in Brandon and Luke's last in Kelowna.

"It was very hard having them leave home at 15 or 16," said Jeff Schenn. "I had a very good bond with them, but seeing them leave for something like that at 15 is pretty incredible. You think they're grown up because they're 6-feet tall, but you still hope they miss home. I know they do. Not as much now. When Luke went to Kelowna he had the most amazing billets (Barry and Ingrid Davidson).

"(Former Rockets star) Tyler Myers (Buffalo Sabres) was there, he billeted at the same place as Luke. Shea Weber (Nashville Predators), Carsen Germyn (Calgary Flames, now playing in Europe), Mikael Backlund (Flames) was the last guy, then they shut it down and (the Davidsons) aren't taking billets anymore. They used to have a 'Rocket Room' in the basement; they're very good people. It's amazing that the five billets they had turned out to be pros."

Brayden finished his junior career in Saskatoon, after the Blades acquired him for a late-season push in 2010–11; he got to live at home for his final few months as an amateur.

He appreciates the chance to finally play on the same team with his big brother.

"Luke and I are living in the same condominium complex now (in Philadelphia)," said Brayden. "Back in the Kelowna-Brandon days we played against each other and didn't really get to see each other. Now it's nice that our family can come see us and we can all spend the weekend together. I know our parents love it, our sisters do and we do, too. It's pretty cool being able to play in the NHL with your brother on the same team. I was pumped when I found out he was coming to Philadelphia. He was excited as well."

The Schenns' parents and sisters, indeed, had just visited the boys in Philadelphia before the Flyers headed out on the road trip that took them to Winnipeg. It was their second family reunion in the City of Brotherly Love; there might have been more family visits but because of the lockout that wiped out the first portion of the 2012–13 season, the boys had spent plenty of time during the summer, autumn and early winter at home in Saskatoon.

Currently in the NHL there are only a handful of same-team brother acts. Beside the Saskatoon Schenns the list includes identical twins Henrik and Daniel Sedin, who were selected back to back in the first round of the 1999 draft by the Vancouver Canucks; they had been teammates in Sweden and have continued primarily as linemates since being drafted. Jordan Staal, a Stanley Cup winner with the 2009 Pittsburgh Penguins, joined his older brother Eric Staal, a Stanley Cup winner with the 2006 Carolina Hurricanes, following a 2012 trade. The Hurricanes also own the NHL rights of Jared Staal, the youngest of the four brothers from Thunder Bay, Ontario, a family group that includes New York Rangers defenceman Marc Staal. Jared made his NHL debut in April, 2013. In 2012, Jordie Benn joined his younger brother Jamie Benn, a product of Victoria who played junior in Kelowna, on the roster of the Dallas Stars. Jordie Benn did not play major junior hockey, but he did play junior A in British Columbia. Jamie Benn and Luke Schenn were teammates for one season with the Rockets.

There have been many family acts in the NHL, including numerous sets of brothers on the same team. The list of Saskatchewan brothers who played together includes Max, Doug and Reg Bentley of Delisle, who played together on a forward line for the Chicago Blackhawks in 1943; Richie and Robyn Regehr, who were born abroad as sons of Mennonite missionaries before growing up in Rosthern and spending a short stint as teammates with the Calgary Flames in 2005–07; Regina-born brothers Ernie and Bill Hicke spent the 1970–71 season as teammates with the California Golden Seals; Bill Kyle of Dysart played three games with the New York Rangers between 1949–51 when his older brother Gus was on the same team; and Don and Nick Metz of Wilcox played virtually their entire careers together with the Maple Leafs.

There are other brother combinations who have just missed each other in the NHL, including Dwight King and his still-active older brother D.J., who are from Meadow Lake and played consecutively for the WHL's Lethbridge Hurricanes but as yet haven't been NHL teammates, nor have Peter and Nolan Schaefer of Yellow Grass; Grant and Bill Warwick of Regina had extensive pro careers in the minor leagues, but Grant played nine seasons in the NHL that started with being named the league's top rookie in 1941–42, and for part of the 1943–44 season they were teammates with the Rangers; Ken Smith, born in Moose Jaw, played from 1944–51 with Boston and his brother Don, born in Regina, spent part of 1949–50 with the Rangers; Tony Leswick of Humboldt had a 12-year NHL career, highlighted by a game-winning, overtime goal that gave Detroit a seventh-game victory over Montreal in the 1954 Stanley Cup final. Tony Leswick started in 1945, basically when older brother Pete was done in the NHL and more than a decade after another brother, Jack, died mysteriously following a one-year career with Chicago; Sheldon and Wade Brookbank of Lanigan, Colby and Riley Armstrong of Saskatoon and Gordie and Vic Howe of the Saskatoon area had NHL careers that overlapped without playing together on the same team.

Rocky Trottier of Climax played from 1983–85 with the New Jersey Devils, but played only against his Hall of Fame brother Bryan; brothers Drew and Jock Callander, of Regina, were too far apart in age to have played together; injuries ended the career of Quill Lake's Selmar Odelein before his younger brother Lyle played in the NHL; Barrie Meissner, born in Unity, and his brother Dick Meissner, born in Kindersley, didn't play in the NHL at exactly the same time, nor did brothers Joby and Mitch Messier from Regina, Todd and Jeff Nelson of Prince Albert or Gene and Dennis Sobchuk of Lang; and Otto and Jackie Schmidt, from Odessa, didn't play together during their brief NHL careers, nor did Saskatoon's Fred and Gord Williams.

The Schenn brothers, like many of their provincial mates, feel a kinship to other Saskatchewan born players.

"Most nights you can look across and, even if the guy's older than you or you don't really know him, I feel like every Saskatchewan guy is tied into you," said Luke Schenn. "You always know that guy through someone; it's just typical of Saskatchewan, where everyone kind of knows everybody. You look across and give him a little nod sometimes. Obviously Saskie guys have respect for each other and we know who they are: (Winnipeg's James) Wright, (Montreal's Travis) Moen, (Columbus' Blake) Comeau...The odd guy might sneak through because he went to college, like Tyler Bozak. In Toronto it was me, Bozak, Keith Aulie, Colby Armstrong hanging out together, the Saskatchewan guys. We also had Clarke MacArthur (of Lloydminster), Colton Orr (of Winnipeg), Joffrey Lupul (of Fort Saskatchewan, Alberta) and James Reimer (of Morweena, Manitoba). When we had dad's trips through Boston and New York, our dads would get invited along. The dads from Saskatchewan would be hanging out with together. All western guys, talking about things they had in common, farming, the weather, asking about what's going on down in Regina, how are things in Lloyd and how's the oil."

"Everywhere you look, most teams do have a Saskatchewan guy on them," said Brayden. "It's good to see that Saskatchewan is producing players and hopefully continues on with that. In Saskatchewan the colder winters have something to do with it, a lot of outdoor hockey. That's what helped us. We played a lot of that, also the hard-working, blue-collar attitude.

"When you start listing Saskatchewan names like Gordie Howe, those are some big names right there. Obviously you want to work your way up, you want to represent Saskatchewan well. There's a lot of good people from there and you want to make them proud."

The brothers also haven't forgotten where they started their minor hockey careers — in Saskatoon.

"I don't know what it is right now," says Luke Schenn, "but there's lots of Saskatoon guys: James Wright, who we're playing today, Darcy Kuemper, Carter Ashton had the same background as us. There's a lot of Saskatchewan guys out there. I'm hoping they keep on producing. I think Saskatoon Minor Hockey does a good job, Sask First does a good job too and so does Hockey Canada. As a young guy that's the first big experience you get, with Sask First, the first taste of what it's like to try to make it somewhere."

The website Quanthockey.com shows 11 Saskatoon-born players were on NHL rosters in 2013, led by 34-year-old Calgary Flames defenceman Cory Sarich (recently traded). That same website claims 80 Saskatoon-born players have appeared in the National Hockey League. Because Regina and Saskatoon have a running feud, it's noteworthy that Saskatchewan's capital city has produced 87 NHLers.

Well-travelled forwards Brent Ashton and Bobby Schmautz were the most prolific scorers of the Saskatoon bunch. Ashton had been a burly but not overly aggressive, high-scoring junior with the Saskatoon Blades before embarking on a 14-year NHL career in which he was traded nine times. A second-round draft choice of Vancouver in 1976, Ashton would eventually divide 998 regular-season games between the Canucks, Colorado Rockies, New Jersey Devils, Minnesota North Stars, Quebec Nordiques, Detroit Red Wings, Winnipeg Jets, Boston Bruins and Calgary

Flames. Ashton recorded 284 goals and 345 assists. Ashton's son Carter, who was born in Winnipeg, was a first-round selection in the 2009 draft; his rights were dealt in 2012 from Tampa Bay to Toronto.

Schmautz, a hard shooter, scored 271 goals and had 286 assists in 764 regular-season games starting in 1967 with the Chicago Blackhawks. Schmautz's career continued with Vancouver, Boston, Edmonton, Colorado, and ending, in 1981, with another stop in Vancouver.

Darren Veitch, who played junior hockey for the Regina Pats and got drafted in 1980's first round by the Washington Capitals, led all Saskatoon-born defencemen in career scoring when he retired in 1991 after additional stops with Detroit and Toronto. A power-play specialist from his junior days, Veitch had 48 goals and 209 assists in 511 regular-season games.

Also among that group from Saskatoon is Hall of Famer Harry "Whipper" Watson, whose 14-year NHL career began in 1941–42 with the Brooklyn Americans, a team that disbanded after that season. Watson was drafted by the Detroit Red Wings and won a Stanley Cup the next year before a two-year break to serve in the Royal Canadian Air Force, before returning to the NHL to win four more Stanley Cups with the Toronto Maple Leafs. Because Gordie Howe's birthplace is Floral — though he grew up in Saskatoon — Watson is the lone Hall of Famer from the "Bridge City."

From Nokomis, north of Regina, Elmer Lach won three Stanley Cups. He also won two scoring titles and the Hart trophy as the league's most valuable player. He was elected to the Hall of Fame in 1966.

PATHWAYS TO
THE HALL OF FAME

Gordie Howe is from Saskatchewan. For his contributions
to the game Howe is known as Mr. Hockey, a title that is trade-
marked. For argument's sake, let's say Howe is the best all-around
player in hockey history. He played 32 seasons of professional
hockey and may be the centrepiece of an illustrious group of Hall
of Famers from the same province. Also from Saskatchewan are
Elmer Lach of Nokomis, Glenn Hall of Humboldt, Bryan Trottier
of Val Marie, Johnny Bower of Prince Albert, brothers Max and
Doug Bentley of Delisle, Eddie Shore of Fort Qu'Appelle, Clark
Gillies of Moose Jaw, Bernie Federko of Foam Lake, Fernie Flaman
of Dysart, Sid Abel of Melville, Bryan Hextall of Grenfell, Bert
Olmstead of Sceptre, Chuck Rayner of Sutherland, Clint Smith of
Assiniboia and Harry Watson of Saskatoon.

Flaman was a space-clearing, physical defenceman who played
900 NHL games with the Boston Bruins and Toronto Maple Leafs,
winning a Stanley Cup in 1951 and ultimately becoming a natu-
ralized U.S. citizen as he turned his attention to coaching. Trottier,

a six-time Stanley Cup champion with the New York Islanders and Pittsburgh Penguins, also became a U.S. citizen so he could represent the country where he played professionally. Gillies, a Memorial Cup winner with the junior Regina Pats, won four Stanley Cups as one of Trottier's teammates with the Islanders.

Federko, a superstar with the junior Saskatoon Blades, began a 14-year NHL career in 1976 with the St. Louis Blues. Federko, as of this book's writing, and Gillies are Saskatchewan's newest Hockey Hall of Famers, getting inducted in 2002.

The first Saskatchewan player inducted into the Hockey Hall of Fame was Shore, who learned to play hockey while growing up tending to horses on a ranch near the town of Cupar. Shore was in the Hall's second class of inductees, getting enshrined in 1947 for a 14-year career spent primarily as a rugged but offensively skilled defenceman with the Bruins. Shore won two Stanley Cups and four times won the Hart Trophy as the NHL's most valuable player before retiring in 1940 to concentrate on operating his American Hockey League franchise, the Springfield Indians.

According to the Hockey Hall of Fame, 17 of the 255 players it inducted before 2013 were born in Saskatchewan. While the remaining inductees come from every corner of North America — and recently from Europe — many of the Saskatchewanians' stories are eerily familiar, growing up on the windswept Prairies, skating on any available patch of ice, whether it was a river, a slough, a schoolyard rink or, if they were lucky, an indoor arena.

"We were pretty fortunate because we had an indoor rink in Nokomis," said Elmer Lach, a 1966 Hockey Hall of Fame inductee who was born in 1918 in Nokomis, a Saskatchewan town of

440 residents about 130 kilometres north of Regina. "We used to play on a curling rink, with the circles on it. It was a church league. Of course, most of our games were played on weekends.

"The manager of the rink in my time helped us a lot. He taught us how to play. We had to buy our own equipment, but there wasn't a (sporting goods) store for us in Nokomis. My mother made a lot of my clothes."

Although cars were common throughout Canada in the 1920s, the Depression hit Saskatchewan especially hard during the next decade. By the Dirty '30s, a moniker earned for the dust storms that wiped out the province's farm crops, many people in Saskatchewan couldn't afford gasoline to operate their vehicles. So they hooked their cars to horses, used them as wagons and dubbed them "Bennett Buggies" or "Anderson Carts" in deference to Canadian Prime Minister Richard Bennett and Saskatchewan Premier James Anderson. Hence, Lach and his young teammates didn't have vans or buses in which to ride to games in the towns surrounding Nokomis. The roads were mainly gravel and there was always the cold, the snow and winter storms to deal with on their cross-country excursions.

"Our transportation was a team of horses," said Lach. "When we got cold, we got off the sleigh and ran beside the horses. Our competition was always the small-town neighbours from Strasbourg and Govan, too. There was a guy who lived northwest of us, Lemberger, (he) was the manager, he looked after the transportation. My uncle lived not too far from the village; he had horses, they were pacers and they pulled the sled."

Lach played in the National Hockey League from 1940 until

1954. He was the centre on the "Punch Line" with right winger Maurice Richard and left winger Toe Blake, who would later
coach the Canadiens. Lach's playmaking skills helped Richard
become the first NHLer to score 50 goals in a season, which oc-
curred in 1944–45, when Lach's 56 assists and 80 points led the
league. Lach would have won the Art Ross Trophy except that the
former NHL player, coach and general manager whose name is on
the trophy, didn't begin presenting it to the league's top scorer until 1947–48. Lach was still the first winner of the Art Ross Trophy,
when he tallied 30 goals and 31 assists in 1947–48, a year after
recovering from a fractured skull.

Richard would eventually surpass Lach as the NHL's all-time
scoring leader. In turn, Howe would surpass Richard and Wayne
Gretzky would surpass Howe.

For his performance in 1944–45, Lach won the Hart Memorial
Trophy as the player deemed most valuable to his team. Imagine
that! Lach was chosen for the award ahead of Richard, a fiery
competitor who scored 50 goals in 50 games and was an icon
among the French-speaking fans of the Canadiens.

Noted as a gentleman, Lach's low-key demeanour made him a
popular teammate. He was an exceptionally fast skater, adept at
flipping passes to teammates while flying up-ice, and he also drew
accolades for his defensive work.

On Jan. 22, 2013, Lach turned 95; the oldest living former
NHLer and his old team bound together by loyalty and an illustrious history together that nearly didn't occur because the future Hall
of Famer was originally slated to join the Toronto Maple Leafs.

"I guess I was a throw-off of the Leafs'," said Lach. "In my era, we never knew who we belonged to. When we reported to Toronto, (Conn) Smythe ran the team, and he told us he was disappointed in the condition we were in and how small we were. I guess I was the smallest of the group. There was something about me... I never liked him after that. All those little things that rub you, you never forget them. Smythe and I, when we were out in public, would call me 'Lach' and that's it. He never called me by my first name. As I got to know him, he knew what he was doing.

"If the Leafs made a mistake, it was a good mistake for me. Making the team was my big ambition. The Canadiens, they look after you. If you got sick after you retired, you could always go back to them and they would tell you where you were going and who your physician is. Even today I talk to (Canadiens assistant general manager Larry Carrière) once in a while. If I get sick he tells me what physician I'm going to. They were always interested in you, even after you weren't playing."

In his 14 seasons, all with the Canadiens, Lach played 664 games, scored 215 goals, had 408 assists and his 623 regular-season points were a league record when he retired. Lach also won Stanley Cups in 1944, 1946 and 1953 — scoring the overtime, Cup-winning goal against the Boston Bruins in the final championship — while recording 19 goals and 45 assists for 64 points in 76 playoff games.

Early in the lockout-shortened, 2012–13 NHL season, Pittsburgh Penguins superstar Sidney Crosby surpassed Lach's regular-season total and bumped the Hall of Famer into 270th all-time on a list of the league's scoring leaders, which is topped by Gretzky (2,857 points), Mark Messier (1,887) and Howe (1,850).

When he was a teenager, Lach tried playing junior hockey.

By the 1930s, junior hockey was becoming a major sport in Saskatchewan. All the best, young players were joining junior teams like the Regina Pats, Moose Jaw Canucks, Saskatoon Wesleys and Weyburn Wanderers. Lach admitted he was a late-comer to hockey, so he wasn't proficient enough to play junior hockey with the young stars and was instead, at the beginning, relegated to playing senior hockey in Weyburn and Regina. Playing against men was actually a blessing in disguise, Lach said, because it made him stronger and taught him how to leverage the puck away from bigger, physically superior opponents, while managing to avoid their crushing hits. Lach also crossed paths with some of the six Bentley brothers from Delisle, including the two who would eventually be enshrined with him in the Hockey Hall of Fame.

"There was a guy from the east named Gizzy Hart, he played (for the NHL's Detroit Cougars and Montreal Canadiens), he helped us a lot, he also coached us (with the senior Weyburn Beavers)," said Lach. "I played with Johnny England, stayed with him, that's where they located me. I finally got a tryout with a team in Saskatoon. I was pretty young. I was 14 or 15, I couldn't make the junior team, I wasn't good enough.

"Doug Bentley and his brother also played senior hockey. They were great skaters. Max was good with the puck. Doug was the older brother; we chummed around a lot.

"If you look at it, all the best players came from Saskatchewan."

After playing minor hockey in Saskatchewan, Doug and Max Bentley were teammates with the Chicago Blackhawks in the 1940s. Undersized, but fast and deft stickhandlers, they were frequently linemates and, for a short span in 1942–43 were joined on a Blackhawks forward unit by their youngest brother Reggie, helping Doug lead the league in scoring. Doug had six seasons with 20 or more goals, but was mired on a bad team before being reunited with Max on the New York Rangers. Max wasn't as tenacious a back-checker as his older brother, but his puck-handling abilities earned him the nickname "Dipsy-Doodle Dandy from Delisle." Doug was inducted into the Hall in 1964; Max went in two years later.

Abel, a teammate of Howe's in Detroit, was enshrined in 1969, the same year as Hextall. Abel joined the Red Wings in 1938 and, after playing his final two seasons in Chicago following a trade from Detroit, retired in 1954. A three-time Stanley Cup champion who would form part of the "Production Line" with linemates Howe and Ted Lindsay, Abel also had success as a coach and administrator.

Hextall grew up in Manitoba before joining the New York Rangers as a left-shooting right winger, a novelty at the time. Hextall scored 187 goals in 11 seasons, plus his overtime marker against the Maple Leafs won the 1940 Stanley Cup for New York, the last championship for the Blueshirts before they finally won again in 1994.

Olmstead, whose hard-checking ways against stars like Howe earned the respect of linemates Lach, Richard, Boom Boom Geoffrion and Jean Beliveau, won four Stanley Cups with the Canadiens during the 1950s before becoming a playing-coach with the Maple Leafs and winning another championship with Toronto. Like Olmstead, Watson was also lauded for his leadership abilities.

Watson spent time with four NHL teams between 1941–54, winning one Stanley Cup with Detroit and four with Toronto.

Saskatchewan's Hall of Famers include some of hockey's most legendary players and a group of goalies in Bower, Hall and Rayner whose exploits make them among the best-known puck-stoppers in the history of hockey. Bower started playing hockey with goalie pads hand-made by a friend and a stick his dad carved from a tree branch, but he endured 25 professional seasons. Rayner moved from his hometown of Sutherland into nearby Saskatoon before advancing to the NHL and becoming one of five goalies to ever win the Hart Trophy, in 1949–50 with the Rangers, as the league's most valuable player. Rayner never felt tethered to the net and introduced the idea of a goalie leaving his crease to handle the puck.

Hall gained notoriety for his nerves because, despite his experience and ability, he was known to vomit before every game. During a 20-year pro career that ended in 1971 at the age of 40, Hall became known as Mr. Goalie, was credited with pioneering the "butterfly style" of falling to his knees and kicking out his pads, plus he owns the record of playing 532 consecutive NHL games as a goalie. From his first appearance as a professional, Hall remembers being accepted, even welcomed, because of his Saskatchewan heritage.

"I think there always has been a bond if you're from Saskatchewan," said Hall. "Now that you mention it and I never thought about it before, but one of the Warwicks — it was Billy's brother (Grant, who like Bill Warwick advanced from Regina to a solid NHL career) — I was playing my first year of pro in Indianapolis in the American League. He was playing on another team, but he knew I was from Saskatchewan. He came by, gave me a little tap on the ass and said, 'Keep it going and good luck.' I remember that was the first deal. Saskatchewan people, we know our roots. I don't think anybody from Saskatchewan is afraid of hard work.

"We were lucky to have Leo Parker in Humboldt," continued Hall, recounting a long-time amateur hockey booster who earned enshrinement into the Saskatchewan Sports Hall of Fame and whose name adorned the town's old hockey rink. "We got a little coaching from some of the schoolteachers who lent their time to us. We weren't over-coached because now you wonder about the over-coaching and the year-round hockey. I would have found that impossible. If you're playing and it's not fun, how are you going to play well? The season wasn't that long. I remember putting the skates on my bike, hooking them on, then riding out to the slough. Most of the time I was there alone, but on weekends we had a crowd. In those days our hair was blowing back. Now I don't follow hockey that much, mind you, in the travelling through the little towns we look to see who's from the little towns. I've got a daughter in Kelvington, so I drive through Saskatchewan to visit her. My biggest problem now is driving to the cemetery so I can visit all my friends.

"Of course we played on the sloughs when we were growing up. That was the only place we could get sometimes. We were lucky in Humboldt — we could get public skating from 4 til 6 on the indoor rink every day. On Saturday we got our hockey. We didn't get a lot of hockey, but we got our hockey. Our skating improved. We had the sloughs until the snow came. Shinny was absolutely part of our life.

"Johnny (Bower) and I were the goalkeepers in action. I knew John's history, where he came from, the great career he had. When we were growing up we knew about the Bentleys certainly, they were big names at the time. Metro Prystai (of Yorkton) played in those days; he was a top junior in the west for years and years until Gordie (Howe) came along."

Howe's path to greatness actually started between the pipes. That's right, the world's best right-winger initially planned to be a goaltender.

"Gord started out as a goaltender in school," said Howe's younger brother, Vic Howe, who also advanced from Saskatoon to play in the National Hockey League — 33 games with the New York Rangers between 1950–55. "He was good. All the public schools had their own teams. We used to go to school in the mornings and the teacher would say, 'OK, get out of here.' So the two of us would go down, play hockey, then go back to school. He was a goalie as a pee wee hockey player, but he was always getting hurt, not on the ice.

"We were at a friend's place, waiting for them to come out because we were going to go downtown for something. We were out in the garage when he started jumping, trying to get a hold of the rafter. He couldn't make it, so he got a bench, got on the bench, took a big leap, missed the rafter with his hand and it caught him right across the forehead. He turned straight up and down, came down on his head and I thought, 'That looks funny!' He was a little crazy. After he hit his head the people we were waiting for came out, so I took off across the field to let our mother know.

I came back, and this was at 8 o'clock on a Saturday morning. We got back to the house and got a car to take him to the hospital. He didn't regain consciousness until 5 or 6 o'clock Monday evening. Saturday, Sunday and then Monday around suppertime he came out of it. He did stupid things."

Gordie Howe has always been one of hockey's great ambassadors, willing to sign autographs and meet with fans at any function. His approachable persona developed when he was playing for the Detroit Red Wings in the 1960s and he became a spokesman for Eaton's department stores, endorsing WinnWell and Truline hockey equipment. It carried through his career and into his retirement.

"We all know about Gordie Howe," said James Wright, a forward from Saskatoon who played junior hockey for the Vancouver Giants and joined the Winnipeg Jets in 2013. "I didn't know Bryan Trottier is from Saskatchewan — that shames me. Gordie Howe is from northern Saskatchewan. He was a part-owner of the Vancouver Giants, so I met him. Very nice, a really nice guy. We know about Gordie Howe."

Unfortunately, Gordie Howe was suffering from dementia while this book was being written. One of his sons, Marty Howe, politely declined having his dad participate in this project because of Gordie's failing memory, directing questions instead to Vic Howe. Newspaper reports revealed Gordie Howe to be quite at ease when fishing, doing errands around his house and even in social settings. In March, 2013, the Vancouver Giants honoured Howe's 85th birthday with a party before one of their Western Hockey League games. Former NHL stars Bobby Hull, Dennis Hull and Johnny Bower were among the guests. Howe looked comfortable when kibitzing with fans, especially the young hockey players in attendance, but his memory apparently faltered when asked for specifics about his illustrious career. Howe's wife, Colleen, died in 2009 from Pick's disease, a form of mental illness. Colleen had long served as her husband's quasi-agent, a financial advisor after Howe realized in the 1960s that he was an underpaid superstar making less than $50,000 annually while less-worthy teammates were making twice his salary.

Howe's family revealed his dementia when it became obvious in his public appearances, specifically when his son Mark Howe was inducted into the Hockey Hall of Fame in 2011.

Six times Howe was chosen as the NHL's most valuable player. Twelve times he was chosen a first-team all-star; he played in the NHL all-star games 23 times. Six times he was the league's scoring leader. He won four Stanley Cups. His NHL career began in the 1940s and ended in the 1980s, making him the first NHLer to play in five decades. He played with the World Hockey Association's Houston Aeros from 1973–77, before moving with his sons Marty and Mark to the New England Whalers for two seasons. When four WHA teams joined the NHL in 1979–80, Howe played one more NHL season, playing all 80 games for the Whalers and tallying 41 points on 15 goals and 26 assists. He was 52 when he retired. Seventeen seasons later, when he was 69, Howe signed a one-game contract with the International Hockey League's Detroit Vipers, playing one shift, thus becoming the only hockey player to play professionally in six decades.

In 1,767 NHL games he scored 801 goals and added 1,049 assists for 1,850 points. He also had 1,685 penalty minutes.

In 157 playoff games he had 68 goals, 92 assists, 160 points and 220 penalty minutes. Admittedly the WHA was an inferior league, but playing there between the ages of 45–51, Howe dressed for 419 regular-season games, scored 174 goals, added 334 assists, totalled 508 points and had 399 penalty minutes. Howe also played 78 WHA playoff games, totalling 71 points on 28 goals and 43 assists, with 115 penalty minutes. And he won two Avco Cups by winning consecutive WHA championships with Houston.

The world's best all-around hockey player was born in Floral, Saskatchewan, on the outskirts of Saskatoon. The tiny village no longer exists, having been swallowed by Saskatoon, which has named a street on its outskirts after Howe's birthplace, and the growing city now claims Howe as its own. A statue of Howe sits outside the Credit Union Centre, home of the Western Hockey League's Saskatoon Blades. Unlike the statue immortalizing Howe inside Joe Louis Arena, where his long-time NHL team, the Detroit Red Wings, plays, the statue in Saskatoon makes Howe look scrawny, cold and isolated on Saskatchewan's flat landscape.

Shortly after Gordie Howe was born in 1928, his family moved into the city, where Howe later began skating on the frozen South Saskatchewan River hour after hour, naturally honing the skills that ultimately made him the National Hockey League's leading scorer.

"There was a big difference between Gord's size and my size," said Vic Howe. "And he was out skating for most of the 24 hours in each day, often on the Saskatchewan River, which ran right through Saskatoon. The city would plow that and flood that part of the river every year. It was twice the size of a hockey rink and there would be 20 guys on each team. If he wasn't playing there he was at the school, which was half a block away from our house. On the road that went by our place they used to haul ice out of the river and the trucks would drive right by our place and the school, and you'd swear to God it was the earth shaking.

"Everybody would laugh about mom putting books on the floor. It was a couple hundred yards to the rink, so at lunchtime he would skate to the house, come inside, have lunch, and he didn't have to take his skates off because she had placed books on the floor to walk on with our skates. Afterward he would turn around and go back out. I was skating, too, but not that much at that time because I was a little runt. To give you an idea, he went to Omaha (to play minor-pro hockey) when he was 16 and he was crowding the 6-foot mark."

Gordie Howe was more than just a scorer — he was a dominating and fearless player who could overpower opponents and wasn't adverse to fighting when required.

NHL players have to play with a reckless abandon, a fearlessness that allows them to block shots, crash into other players, drive to the net and not worry about being injured. Howe was usually inflicting the injuries. Opponents spoke reverentially about his flying elbows, his strength and his fighting ability.

"We stayed in pretty good shape," said Vic Howe, recalling his and Gordie's childhood. "Our dad was working with the city and they were pouring sidewalks. They had a big mixer. A bag of cement weighed 88 pounds. (Gord) would go over, haul two, rip them open, throw the stuff in then work the cement around. If you work like that all day you would get strong. One of the guys he worked with had a truck, so he used to go out in the evenings, picking up loads for people. Gord would go out and shovel gravel or whatever for four hours after supper. The strength was there. Our grandfather was 6-foot-2 and strong as a bull, our father was just plain strong. Gord would go away, come back and work that way in the summer. I'd go away, come back and go to work on the golf course.

"Glenn Hall played, Johnny Bower. I think it was a case of the Saskatchewan players being in better condition because the other guys had the rinks with a roof on them. We were playing on the outdoor rinks. One example, when we were playing juvenile, the playoffs started and we were playing against a team about 25 miles west of Saskatoon. We were playing a two-game, total-goal series. They arrived in Saskatoon and we played on the inside rink; we beat them 24–0. We were supposed to go back there the following Saturday. We were up 24 goals but had to go to their rink, which was outdoors. It was 26-below, with a wind; it was wide open, snow was piled up all around the rink. Believe it or not there was 220 people there, standing on the snowdrifts. We were a little smarter. They had a little shed there, so we dressed two goaltenders — they would change each line change. When we'd change goaltenders the people around the rink would go inside to get warm. We beat them 12–0. Over 200 people standing up on those snowdrifts in the cold! Our manager called, trying to get them to cancel it. They said, 'We can't cancel it. We've sold tickets.'

"When it comes to hockey there were all kinds of Saskatchewan guys around, but they come from covered rinks now."

Saskatchewan doesn't just prepare players for the Hockey Hall of Fame. Of the first 100 builders inducted into the Hockey Hall of Fame before 2013, six were born in Saskatchewan — Keith Allen of Saskatoon, Jack Butterfield of Regina, Clarence Campbell of Fleming, Ed Chynoweth of Dodsland, Emile Francis of North Battleford and Gordon Juckes of Watrous. Strangely enough, of the 15 officials inducted into the Hall of Fame, none are from Saskatchewan. The paucity of officials is easily explained — the NHL's six original franchises were located in eastern Canada and the U.S., so that's where the league gathered its officials from. As the NHL expanded across North America it needed more officials, so the league started recruiting from elsewhere; any of those worthy officials will be duly enshrined in the future. Referees Mick McGeough, Brad Watson and Mike Hasenfratz, all of Regina, and linesman Mark Wheler of North Battleford are among the NHL's recent and current on-ice officials.

Allen was the first head coach of the Philadelphia Flyers, subsequently becoming the general manager who designed the Broad Street Bullies into Stanley Cup champions. Butterfield, a nephew of Eddie Shore, was a long-time president of the American Hockey League. Campbell served as NHL president from 1946–77. Chynoweth spent 23 years as president of the Western Hockey League, ending in 1996, and concurrently for 20 years as president of the Canadian Major Junior Hockey League. After 13 years playing professionally as a goalie, Francis became a junior coach before advancing to coaching and managerial jobs with the New York Rangers, St. Louis Blues and Hartford Whalers. Juckes was primarily involved with amateur hockey inside Saskatchewan, although much of his work had international ramifications with the International Ice Hockey Federation and Canadian Olympic Committee.

Weyburn's Tiger Williams was one of the most colourful hockey players to ever lace up a pair of skates. He is the all time career leader in penalty minutes.

ROADS TO
THE PROS

" "**H**i, it's Tiger."

No other description. Just an enthusiastic voice on the other end of the telephone, speaking with a bit of a lisp, saying he was eager to meet for a discussion about NHL players from Saskatchewan. He's one of the most famous and popular Saskatchewan NHLers — Dave "Tiger" Williams, born in Weyburn, played major junior hockey with Swift Current and professionally for five NHL teams during 14 seasons — Toronto Maple Leafs, Vancouver Canucks, Detroit Red Wings, Los Angeles Kings and Hartford Whalers. Nobody calls him "Dave" or "David" or "Mr. Williams." He's been "Tiger" seemingly forever, since a minor-hockey coach in his Saskatchewan home town decided that nickname best described the persona of the five-year-old fireball.

Williams progressed through minor hockey and took the well-travelled path to the NHL that led him through the rough-and-tumble era of the Western Canada Hockey League (later the WHL). That path to the NHL is still available. Indeed, the WHL claims it has produced 20 per cent of the players on NHL rosters. But checking the pedigrees of pro players these days it's evident that many chose other routes, including circumventing Canada's three major-junior hockey leagues and instead heading to an American university, where the student-athletes have the option of getting an education before turning pro. That wasn't a path Williams pondered from his childhood. He just wanted to play hockey. One of his brothers insists that Williams, upon being told he had a tryout with a junior team in Saskatoon, jumped on his bicycle and pedalled the 350 kilometres from Weyburn. It's such a great story and so perfectly describes Tiger, we're not going to get it confirmed or denied.

"We lived right on the river in Weyburn — the Souris River," said Williams. "From our backyard it was down the bank and onto the river. My brother, Morgan, fell into the river, so that was the end of the river. We moved that summer.

"We'd be lucky to have 10 to 12 kids out there playing in the winter. That part of Weyburn was by the old mental hospital. The Souris ran through town. That was skid row, right where we lived. That was every fucking DP (displaced person), that's where they lived. My old man was one of those. The kids who had skates, or could steal skates, skated down there. I always remember always having skates, a stick. We just had them. We used to like coming into Regina when I was a young kid, you guys in Regina would leave your sticks outside. Well, they're in Weyburn now. We were using those sticks. I could never understand why the guys in Regina would leave four or five sticks in the snowbank in front of their house. That was so nice of them to leave those sticks there for us. I thought they were a provincial stick."

Williams can be the most gregarious guy in the room, visiting and telling stories to everyone in the place. Or, on this day standing at a bar in a downtown Regina restaurant, he can be inconspicuous while wearing a hat, his face covered in a beard and hidden behind a newspaper he's reading voraciously while he waits to get engaged on one of his favourite topics: Saskatchewan.

"When we have a chance to go to junior and get drafted, from that moment on we represent that bus driver, that Zamboni driver, that trainer, that billet and those other teammates. We get to represent them. If you get to represent them for over 1,000 games in a pro league, which I got to do, you can never forget about them. They end up being your deepest supporters, they end up being your after-burners. You feel them behind you, you should feel them. I think most of us Western kids, especially us Saskatchewan kids, I know we all get that. That's what your job is. It seems to me no matter how good you were in junior, or if you went to college, there's a certain group that suddenly decided you're going to go on and play because we think you'll remember us. We're going to push you, we're going to protect you. They were a part of it. One thing I get very, very clearly, is without them I never would have played a single game. The minor hockey system in Weyburn gave me a chance to go to Swift Current. The people in Swift Current gave me an opportunity to go to the next level. I was lucky enough to take it to the very top level. Without those communities and those people, you're shovelling shit at the livestock yards in Weyburn. That's fucking life. And I get that. I never forget that."

Williams is the NHL's all-time leader in penalty minutes,

with 3,966, but he could also score. In 1,045 regular-season and playoff games he had 253 goals and 295 assists. Ten times he scored more than 15 goals in a season, with a career-high of 35 while playing for Vancouver in 1980–81. Dave "The Hammer" Schultz, a Saskatchewan product with the Philadelphia Flyers in 1974–75, holds the record of 472 penalty minutes in one season. Williams led the NHL three times in penalty minutes during a season but his personal high of 358 minutes, set in 1986–87 with Los Angeles, is 17th on the all-time list.

Anyone thinking he's a big buffoon would be wrong. He's an emotional guy, not too big, opinionated and passionate. And one of his favourite subjects is Bryan Trottier, a member of the Hockey Hall of Fame and six-time Stanley Cup winner as a player. Henri "Pocket Rocket" Richard has the NHL record with 11 Stanley Cup victories as a player, all with the Montreal Canadiens between 1956–73. Others won more, but Trottier is one of 17 players with their names etched on the Cup six times. Trottier won four straight times with the New York Islanders between 1980–83 and twice with the Pittsburgh Penguins in 1991 and 1992.

"When I played in the NHL, I never would hang out with players from the other team and I could be pretty mean about players on our team who would be friends with players on the other teams, but Bryan and I had a special friendship," said Williams. "Whenever he would come into town, the night before the game we would get together, but we would always go someplace where I knew nobody would recognize us, someplace the other players never went to. The only reason we did do it was because we didn't want to jeopardize our credibility with our own teammates.

That's asinine as a process, because why would you ever question Trottier's or Williams' ability to perform and try to win every game? It's unfortunate that some people have things like that in their lives: A conflict of interest. If you avoid conflicts of interest you'll have a smoother ride. But it's kind of stupid in a way.

"I used to spend some time at Bryan's place. I was over there one day and wanted to get a drink of water, so I went into the kitchen and couldn't find a tap. I said to him, 'Trots, don't you have running water?' He took me out to the backyard, pointed at the creek that ran past his place and said, 'There — running water!' "

Williams' on-ice flamboyance was personified by riding his hockey stick after scoring a goal. He yelled at opponents, argued with referees and, if he liked you, was fiercely loyal. He was known as an enforcer.

Trottier, as noted earlier, also grew up along a river: Frenchman's Creek ran through his family's land in tiny Val Marie, Saskatchewan. Trottier's father travelled throughout Saskatchewan, so Bryan was born in Redvers, but the family moved onto the Val Marie ranch when he was a kid. That's where the future Hall of Famer first practised his skating and puck-handling. And it's where his career almost ended before it started, if not for his friendship with Williams.

"I was at Hockey Day in Canada in P.E.I.," said Trottier, on the occasion of his induction in 2012 into the inaugural class of the Saskatchewan Hockey Hall of Fame. "We were all telling stories about playing hockey outdoors, playing on ponds, learning how to skate. I told the story about learning to skate on Frenchman's Creek, which is about 150 feet from our front door. My dad would go out there and chop the beaver dam. He would chop the beaver dam at night and the next morning we would have fresh ice. This one Canadian songwriter, I was listening to this, he's from Cape Breton, and he put it so eloquently: 'How iconically Canadian — that in the middle of Saskatchewan, in the middle of winter, a father used a beaver to flood a pond for a future Hall of Famer.'

"I talk about the twists and turns, but my hockey career may have taken a really tough turn and it wouldn't have been OK if not for one guy, and that's Tiger Williams. I may get a little emotional here. I was playing hockey in Swift Current when I was 16 years old. At Christmas time I was so homesick. I was small, 5-foot-6 and 155 pounds, playing against these 6-foot-3 monsters, and I was getting worn ragged, beaten up, lost my two front teeth. I came home for Christmas and my mom makes all my favourite stuff: turkey, mashed potatoes, gravy, and I'm thinking, 'I don't know if I'm going back.' We had a game on Boxing Day. I'm wavering a little bit as Dad says, 'You better get going.' So the phone rings and it's (Swift Current Broncos coach) Stan Dunn. He says, 'Are you coming? We're waiting for you. OK? Practice tomorrow at 10 o'clock.' So now my coach kind of knows, my dad knows, I'll stay here and go to school. Everything will be OK and I won't have to play against those monsters anymore. The next morning at 6:30, maybe quarter to seven, there's a knock on the door. My mom opens the door and says, 'Hey, Tiger, what are you doing here?' Tiger says, 'Hi Mary, what's for breakfast?' 'What do you want?' 'I'll have a couple eggs.'

"I ask him, 'Tiger, what are you doing here?' He told me, 'Coach wants me to come and get you. He's worried about you coming back, so he checked with your dad and told me not to come back without you.' I told Tiger, 'Are you crazy? I'm not going back.' I was still unsure, so I talked to Dad and he said, 'Maybe you should go back. You can always come home.' As a 16-year-old that's what I needed to hear, that I could always come home. So Tiger and I jumped in the car and drove all the way back to Swift Current with him saying, 'Nobody's going to touch you for the rest of the year. I'll be playing with you and nobody's going to touch you.' For the rest of the year I'd be playing and these big guys would be swirling around, but there's Tiger growling at them — 'Grrrrrr!' I'm thinking, 'This is awesome!' "

Trottier was drafted 22nd overall by the Islanders in 1974, Williams was drafted 33rd overall by Toronto in 1974. While Williams started his first pro season with the Oklahoma City Blazers of the Central Hockey League before being summoned midway through to Toronto, Trottier — two years younger than Williams — remained in junior hockey and moved with the Broncos to their new home in Lethbridge, Alberta. Trottier and Williams never again played on the same team, at least until they joined forces on Oldtimers teams, but they met countless times until Williams retired following the 1987–88 season. Trottier retired in 1991–92, but financial problems forced him to come back with Pittsburgh for part of the 1993–94 season.

"Bryan Trottier?" said Williams. "Gordie Howe? Gordie's Gordie, he's Mister Hockey and will always be because he set the bar. You and I are not in the business to compare anybody, but Trottier at the end of the day is Number One. He's won more Cups, accomplished more, come from very, very meagre starts. Some people always want to compare things. I've been to Afghanistan eight times. When you're 11 years old in Afghanistan and you can't feed or water yourself, guess what happens. You die! In Saskatchewan and the west we have a lot of passion in our hearts. If Gordie's Mister Hockey, Bryan's Doctor Hockey."

While Williams has been described as a consummate, popular teammate, always willing to fight their battles, Trottier was called the stabilizing force during the Islanders dynasty on a team that included goalie Billy Smith, defenceman Denis Potvin and Trottier's regular linemates Mike Bossy, the sniper, and Clark Gillies a fearless, bruising winger.

Gillies is a Moose Jaw native who played for the Regina Pats when they beat Swift Current in a playoff series en route to winning the 1974 Memorial Cup as Canada's top junior team.

"I never forget the success we had there, what a stepping stone it was to the NHL," said Gillies, who was drafted fourth overall by the Islanders in 1974. "I was a 15-, 16-year-old kid coming out of Moose Jaw. I didn't even know if I was good enough to play in Regina, for crissakes! To go there and be given such a great opportunity... and I was given an opportunity. I don't mince that at all. I was given a chance to play on the top line, with two of the greatest goal scorers to ever play in the Western Hockey League (Dennis Sobchuk and Mike Wanchuk). I was given an opportunity to make a name for myself.

"As long as I played professional hockey, (winning the Memorial Cup) gave me a chance to bust on somebody: 'Excuse me, anybody here, how many guys' — I'd look around the room and I already knew the answer — 'how many guys in here, anybody, anybody win a Memorial Cup? Ooooo-kay... I was just checking.' I was always using the Memorial Cup thing, especially to bust on some guys who asked if you had ever accomplished anything. 'Anybody here win a Memorial Cup and a Stanley Cup?'

"I've taken that experience with me. I never thought I would like Regina, but I enjoyed it. Growing up it was always, 'Moose Jaw, Moose Jaw, Moose Jaw...' We never liked anybody from Regina. The (senior Moose Jaw) Pla-Mors and the (Regina) Caps. The (junior Moose Jaw) Canucks and the Pats. I never saw the Moose Jaw Civic Centre hopping the way it was when Regina was playing. Everybody was there, and vice versa. That rolled all the way to minor hockey. When we were playing midget hockey against teams from Regina, shit, we wanted to kick their ass. We didn't always do it, but there were memorable games. All of a sudden I get invited to play for the Pats.

"I didn't know how I was going to break it to my folks, but it was easier then because there was no (major junior) team in Moose Jaw at the time. If we had a Western Canada Hockey League team in Moose Jaw, that's where I would have played and I would have been very happy there. It's an example of how problems create opportunities. Not having a team in Moose Jaw was a bit of a problem, but it created a big opportunity for me. God, who knows what would have happened if I had not gone ahead to Regina?"

Playing major junior wasn't even an option for Brett Clark. He played junior A hockey with the Melville Millionaires and was a solid performer who later couldn't crack a major junior roster. The first option of a young player from Wapella was playing junior hockey, but Clark instead ended up on a short-lived scholarship at Maine. After playing one season for the Black Bears, Clark was a

sixth-round draft choice by Montreal in 1996. When Maine's program was suspended for using ineligible players, the Canadiens
dispatched Clark to the Canadian national team for one year
and a stint in the minors before beginning an NHL career that
eventually took him — between more minor-league stops — from
Montreal to Atlanta, Colorado, Tampa Bay and, in 2013, to the
Minnesota Wild.

"It's amazing when you look back at all the guys from this area
(who have played in the NHL) through the years... it could be the
weather," said Clark. "We spend a lot of time indoors at the rinks,
it's a passion.

"I was born in Moosomin, but you better put Wapella in there.
I grew up there on a farm. You learn to respect what they did
and to take advantage of the opportunity. Grain and beef. I had
a few 3-in-the-morning 'C'mon, we've gotta go pull a calf!' Keith
Aulie's like that too, a good guy, very down to earth. Most guys
from Saskatchewan are very down to earth, they know what's gotten them there. You see guys like Jamie Heward, Mike Sillinger,
Wendel Clark.

"My parents ran the rink. I killed a lot of time at the rink. They
were the caretakers when I was growing up. I spent more time
in there when cabarets were on (in the hall beside the rink). My
parents would be there and they couldn't find a babysitter, so I'd
be there with the lights on. That's where the kids go. Sometimes
I had too much access. In Saskatchewan, that's the pastime. Kids
grow up wanting to be in the rinks, especially over the winter
time. In the summer kids do more fishing and other things. Kids
grew up watching senior hockey; the older guys were your heroes.

Every time they'd come out with us there'd be great joy. I remember shovelling snow off the rink because there were no Zambonis. I started skating when I was three, probably started hockey not long after.

"You're seeing more and more Saskatchewan kids going the university route. Some kids aren't quite ready at 20, to make that decision, until they're 21, 22, 23... Some of the junior kids are ready for the NHL, like (Jordan) Eberle, (Steve) Stamkos, (Taylor) Hall. It has a lot to do with how they're brought up."

Gordon "Red" Berenson grew up in Regina, joining the Pats farm system and he seemed destined to be a fixture on the junior team for their games at Exhibition Stadium. He didn't have to leave his home town, but when another option presented itself, he would reject the junior hockey route for an opportunity to play hockey while getting a university education.

"When I was a kid, really a kid, like 11 years old, my mom would wake me up at 5 (a.m.) so I could get to the stadium every Saturday morning," said Berenson. "I knew how to get into the stadium. I would go in there and skate in the dark until the games started at 8. That was my favourite day — I couldn't wait for Saturday morning."

Berenson was recruited by legendary coach Murray Armstrong to join the Pats for their playoff run into the 1955–56 Memorial Cup final, a loss against the Toronto Marlboros. Two years later, after Berenson had scored 95 points for his hometown Pats and Armstrong was coaching Denver University's hockey team, Armstrong tried to recruit Berenson to join him but the gifted scorer instead chose Michigan, a stronger school academically.

"When I opted to go to college, it didn't go over very well," said Berenson. "(Then-Montreal Canadiens general manager) Sam Pollock told me that going to school would ensure that I would never play in the NHL. But I had been told there was no money to be made in the six-team NHL, so some former pros told me to make sure I got an education. I'd say that's about when we started a bit of a pipeline to U.S. colleges."

After an All-America playing career at Michigan, Berenson spent 17 seasons in the NHL, winning a Stanley Cup with Montreal in 1965 before playing with the New York Rangers, St. Louis Blues and Detroit Red Wings. With St. Louis, Berenson appeared in three straight Stanley Cup finals, was voted the West Division's best player and scored six goals in one 1968 game against the Philadelphia Flyers. He retired as a player in 1978 and, after 1 1/2 seasons as an assistant coach, became the Blues' head coach. He was named the NHL's top coach in 1980–81. Since 1984 he's been head coach at the University of Michigan.

Nearly 300 products of U.S. colleges played in the NHL in 2011–12, about 30 per cent of the league's rosters. An unofficial count put the number at 279 in 2013, the lockout-shortened season.

NHL teams can draft players who are at least 18 in the year of their drafting. Most of the draft choices stay with their respective junior or university team for another year or two of experience, before making the jump to pro hockey. American college teams can also offer scholarships to players from anywhere, with few age restrictions, provided they abide by NCAA (National Collegiate Athletic Association) rules. That's how Tanner Glass ended up with a scholarship from Dartmouth College, an Ivy League school in Hanover, New Hampshire.

Glass was born in Regina but surrounding towns were his boyhood homes — he started playing hockey and grew up in Southey until his family moved to Craven and he attended high school in Lumsden, where he made the honour roll. He played midget AAA (17-and-under) with the Yorkton Mallers before spending two junior A seasons in the British Columbia Hockey League and earning a college scholarship. Although Glass is a fast skater and tenacious checker, he's not your typical Ivy Leaguer because he'll play aggressively and fight when required.

"Going to college is a great idea, not only because you get your education paid for but it's good for the kid, too," said Glass. "You've got school responsibilities, looking after your food. When you grow up in Saskatchewan you see that hard work is required to accomplish things, and if you didn't see that your parents would let you know. They would tell you what it's like, that if you don't get an education and you don't make the NHL, you're going to have to work hard."

Glass may have envisioned himself playing senior hockey in southern Saskatchewan, but his skills led him to bigger things. Before heading to Dartmouth in 2003, he was drafted 256th overall by the Florida Panthers — hardly a surefire NHLer. After completing his four years of college eligibility, serving as the Big Green's captain as a senior, he mucked around in the minor leagues between two stints with Florida. An unrestricted free agent in 2009, Glass signed with the Vancouver Canucks and was part of the team that lost the seventh game of the 2011 Stanley Cup final to the Boston Bruins, proving himself to be a bona fide NHL player, although he was more suited to the grinding and penalty-killing roles of a fourth liner. After one season with the Winnipeg Jets, Glass got a two-year contract offer worth $1.1 million annually from the Pittsburgh Penguins and joined them for 2012–13.

"For me it's the guys we started watching, the guys we saw first-hand," said Glass. "Bryan Trottier's a little older, but I do remember watching him with the Penguins. Wendel Clark — I didn't like the Leafs, but I liked watching his style of play, the hits, the fights. My uncles were like that, so this is the way I was taught: You've got to hit, you've got to fight. Wendel's style of play. Selmar Odelein. Most of the Saskatchewan guys are the same. It's never a stretch to say, 'How's it going?' and tap the guy on the shinpads. When they come in you say, 'Hey, you're from Saskatchewan!' "

Whether they're products of junior or college hockey, the tales and the memories are similar.

"I got in trouble one time when I was young and the choice of grounding was two months not going out with my friends or one month of no hockey," said Glass. "I chose two months not going out with my friends. It might have been two weeks instead of two months, but I remember it was double not playing hockey, so I chose the longer one.

"I remember my dad putting me on the slough in the spring-time. He'd pick me up and throw me onto the ice, over the water because it wasn't frozen right to the edge of the slough. I'd be out there skating, hearing the cracks in the ice. If you passed the puck too hard it would slide off the ice and into the water. One year, specifically, and I remember this, I was skating on the ice and I hear this really big 'Crack!' I went as fast as I could, jumped over the water and landed on the other bank. Dad was laughing on the other side. I said, 'Dad, it's not thick enough!' He gave me one of these (shrugs). 'Well, you can swim.' "

Bryan Trottier was a
six-time winner of the
Stanley Cup as a player.
The Hockey News selected
him 30th in its list of the
top 100 players of all time.

GIVING BACK

Hockey players from Saskatchewan never truly and completely leave their home province. If they're playing professionally, of course they physically leave Saskatchewan because the province doesn't have any pro hockey teams. Sometimes they come back to spend summers on family farms, like Keith Aulie does near Rouleau, or they come back to enjoy their off-seasons at Waskesiu Lake in Prince Albert National Park, or fishing along the Saskatchewan River or relaxing at their cottage on one of the Fishing Lakes — Pasqua, Mission, Echo and Katepwa — near Eddie Shore's old stomping grounds of Fort Qu'Appelle and Cupar. They might actually own a house in Saskatoon or Regina, like Brooks Laich does. Sometimes they move away to be closer to where they're playing and return for family visits, special events or off-season workouts, like Blair Jones. Or sometimes, like Mike Sillinger, they return to Saskatchewan after their NHL careers are over because their hearts never left and they feel obliged, perhaps, to give back to the place and people who helped them make it to the NHL. Sillinger does it through the Shooting Stars Foundation, which stages golf fund-raisers, a banquet and a shinny tournament to support registered children's charities.

Sillinger, a Regina Pats product who holds the distinction of being traded nine times and playing for an NHL-record 12 teams, has teamed with long-time friend and Regina product Jamie Heward, who played with seven NHL teams, in their altruistic endeavours. They also recruited fellow Reginan Jordan Eberle of the Edmonton Oilers to help when they're running their fund-raising golf tournaments and annual street-hockey tournament in downtown Regina.

"I love the fact Mike and I are getting a chance to do charity work in the city, helping kids in the community, getting our names out there," said Heward. "Hopefully it's something we can do for a long time. That's one thing (former NHL player) Billy Hicke and (fellow former Pats co-owner) Ted Knight always told us: You need to be part of the community, be proud of where you're from, and you need to help out as many people as you possibly can. That's something that stuck with me and Mike."

Fred Sasakamoose felt similar obligations. He left Saskatchewan for a while to play professional hockey, but he returned and brought home the knowledge of what it takes to make the NHL: Listening, learning and hard work. He shares that knowledge with the people of the Ahtahkakoop First Nation in northern Saskatchewan, where the residents are well aware Sasakamoose was the first Aboriginal to play in the National Hockey League, making his way from the minor-hockey Duck Lake Ducks to the Western Canada Junior Hockey League's Moose Jaw Canucks to the Chicago Blackhawks.

Sasakamoose has served as chief of his band and remained a councillor for 35 years. He teaches young people the traditional ways of hunting, fishing and trapping. He also helps troubled Aboriginals with drug and alcohol addictions. He has operated a hockey school, supports the Beardy's Blackhawks, a reserve-based team comprising primarily First Nation players that plays in the Saskatchewan Midget AAA Hockey League, and he participated on the NHL Ethnic Diversity Task Force.

There are roughly 2,500 Aboriginals registered with the Saskatchewan Hockey Association. From 1993–2001 the best of those players were able to advance to play for a Saskatchewan Junior Hockey League franchise, the Lebret Eagles, a team founded to give opportunities to Aboriginal players. Any First Nations or Métis player given an opportunity can, in some way, thank Sasakamoose, who endured the racist taunts and long odds to become a role model for future generations.

"I realized long after I played that it was important, that I might have opened lots of doors, I might have paved the way for others," said Sasakamoose. "But I didn't think about it then, making $8,500 from the Chicago Blackhawks."

For 11 games at the end of the 1953–54 NHL season, after his Moose Jaw Canucks had been eliminated by the Regina Pats from the WCJHL playoffs, Sasakamoose lived the grandiose lifestyle of an NHL player — trains, nice hotels and good restaurants — after being summoned to join the Blackhawks. He posted six penalty minutes and no points before returning at season's end to northern Saskatchewan.

Sasakamoose talks about the prejudices he faced while playing hockey and he warns of the dangers of drinking, of not knowing how to handle success and money in an unfamiliar world. He also remembers his teammates with the Canucks, who ultimately accepted him regardless of his race, and how long-time minor-leaguer George Hunchuk worked tirelessly with his new friend in Moose Jaw, showing Sasakamoose how to become a better skater and the effort it would take to become a pro. He speaks warmly of Canucks manager George Vogan, who welcomed Sasakamoose into his home and kept the young Indian from running away from the white man's world.

"When they asked me to say grace at (the Saskatchewan Hall of Fame inaugural induction dinner), I thought it was an honour to be there and I thought, all my life, the white man has done me so much good," said Sasakamoose, who indeed said grace in his native tongue. "It's amazing. A week before I came back from Regina, where I had received the Queen's Diamond Jubilee Medal as an award. Senator Bob Peterson and Frank Mahovlich called to tell me I had been nominated for that medal. It made me sit down and think, especially at my age. Let me say there's a class of people, the white people, who made me who I am now — the honours, the Hall of Fame award, the Aboriginal Achievement Award in Ottawa, the medal I just received. Who did that? It was the white people. Maybe I worked hard, but without them I wouldn't be where I am.

"Even at training camp, when I'm 15 years old, going to play junior hockey. 'Wait a minute — where the hell is Moose Jaw?' There I am, 400 miles away from home, a 15-year-old boy, not knowing what the outside world is like or what is out there. Then you're in the showcase of your life because of the one person who believed in you — George Vogan. I lived at his house. I was growing up, getting stronger. My mother never drank, she was a powerful woman, and she was very disciplined. My father drank a little, but he was a disciplined man. He was a logger from Big River. There were a lot of events that happened in my life.

"I had a grandfather who didn't speak. He didn't see me play in the NHL. He would make my sticks out of willow trees, hang them out to dry overnight...

"He taught me to skate before I went to the residential school, where I liked the discipline, I liked the hard work, making me strong by milking cows; it was good for my training going to the National Hockey League. It made a man out of you, it made me who I am today, it helped me go to the National league, the WHL in Moose Jaw; we were very disciplined because we were taught to listen, and we listened well. It took four years of junior hockey, four years of my life in junior hockey, and lots of hard work.

"It's better now, there are lots of opportunities out there now. It's just that we Indian people have the feeling that it's not for us. We're not hungry. You have to feel that way to make the National league. You need training. It requires discipline. You want to be a champion, you want to see the world — it requires a lot of discipline; you have to listen to your coaches and listen to your parents."

The story sounds like a Hollywood script and, coincidentally, Sasakamoose said he has had discussions with filmmakers about making it into a movie. It starts with his grandfather teaching

Freddie, age five, how to skate one year before the youngster was taken away and put in St. Michael's Indian Residential School in Duck Lake. The school's programs were supervised by Catholic priests from Quebec, who would allow the well-behaved, older kids to skate and play hockey. Residential schools were established to teach native Canadian children the culture, language and lifestyle of the whites, to the point where Sasakamoose had his braided hair cut off, wasn't allowed to visit his family and nearly had his Cree heritage wiped from his memory. Sasakamoose admits the students were abused and tells how difficult that was to overcome, but he believes the discipline being taught actually helped him become a good hockey player.

As a testament to his legacy, Sasakamoose was invited to the ceremonies in Meadow Lake during the summer of 2012 when Los Angeles Kings forward Dwight King brought home the Stanley Cup. It was the Cup's second trip in a decade to Meadow Lake, having been brought there by another home-town hero, Jeff Friesen of the New Jersey Devils, in 2003. After wheeling the Cup around town and before taking it to his family's farm, King honoured his Métis heritage by taking the Cup to visit relatives at the nearby Flying Dust Reserve. King played minor hockey for the Beardy's Blackhawks before progressing to the WHL's Lethbridge Hurricanes. King and Friesen are among a handful of Saskatchewan players with First Nations heritage who have progressed to the NHL. Hall of Famer Bryan Trottier has Cree/Chippewa roots. Theoren Fleury, who was born in Saskatchewan and grew up in Manitoba, has Métis ancestry.

Grant Fuhr, Reggie Leach, Kyle Chipchura, Carey Price, Jordin

Tootoo, Pierre Pilote, George Armstrong and Saskatchewanians Ron Delorme, Wade Redden and Jim Neilson are among the former and current NHLers who have listed First Nations, Inuit or Métis as part of their ancestry. Sasakamoose was the first, but following those 11 games he never regained the conditioning, focus and desire that got him there in the first place. He bounced around the minors inside Canada before returning to Saskatchewan, eventually turning his life in the right direction and becoming a leader, role model and supporter for anyone who wants to heed his advice.

To anyone from outside of Saskatchewan, the province is a bit of a backwater. With barely more than one million residents (about 20 per cent of the population has Aboriginal identity) and only two cities with populations of 200,000-plus, it doesn't have the pizzazz of New York, California, Ontario, Quebec or British Columbia.

"I get teased all the time," said Blair Jones, who grew up in Craik (midway between Regina and Saskatoon) but is a product of Central Butte, a town 100 kilometres northwest of Moose Jaw. "I get called 'Hillbilly' or 'Hick' or get told 'Get off the farm!' It's all in fun. Guys from big cities don't really understand about growing up in Saskatchewan and our idea of fun when we were growing up. They would look at you kind of crazy when you tell them the stupid things you did growing up. They have no idea. Cory Sarich is from just down the road, from Davidson. We joke around about stuff from home. Some of the best times happened in the summer, going to the Craik Dam, camping at the park and going swimming. It was always enjoyable. When the winter rolled back around you were excited to play hockey again."

In the WHL, before being chosen by Tampa Bay in the fourth round of the 2005 draft, Jones played for Red Deer and Moose Jaw. He was sent from his respective NHL team to the minors several times, including the 2013 season, when he was dispatched and recalled by Calgary. His return visits to Saskatchewan usually include off-season workouts and a few days spent with his Moose Jaw billets — Larry and Heather Hoyes.

Sometimes you give back strictly by being proud of where you're from, by defending and/or praising your heritage and sharing your successes. During the NHL lockout of 2012–13, Jones worked out with the Moose Jaw Warriors while awaiting a resolution to the labour dispute and he undoubtedly shared some insight with his former team's younger charges. Jones also comes back to play in fund-raising golf tournaments held throughout the province, where hockey fans and community supporters pay entry fees to golf with well-known NHL players and other celebrities.

Scott Hartnell (Philadelphia Flyers) and Clarke MacArthur (Toronto Maple Leafs) staged their third annual golf tournament in June, 2013, and recruited another co-host from their home city of Lloydminster — Washington Capitals goalie Braden Holtby. Tournament organizers boast that $400,000 was raised in the first two years and donated to the Lloydminster Region Health Foundation, Lloydminster Comprehensive and Holy Rosary high schools and other local charities.

"It's pretty cool," said Hartnell. "You talk to the Schenn brothers, you don't have to ask them twice, it's a guarantee they're going to be there to support your community. I've done the same for them. Jarret Stoll, Nick Schultz, I haven't been to

Keith Aulie's tournament yet. You always make time for that. You can't forget where you come from and the communities that need your support."

Hartnell and MacArthur also successfully applied to the NHL Players' Association for grants through the ongoing Goals & Dreams campaign, one of numerous causes associated with the NHLPA and the NHL itself. Goals & Dreams donated 25 sets of new equipment to Lloydminster's minor hockey program. Tanner Glass of the Pittsburgh Penguins did that a couple of years ago, when he engaged the program to purchase 25 sets of new equipment (valued at $12,500) for Southey, the town 50 kilometres north of Regina where he began playing hockey and his grandfather ran the rink.

"I thought of my grandfather (Emil Boehmer) when I made the donation," Glass said. "He was always at the rink, the guy opening the canteen and making the ice. He wasn't the only one working the canteen though. There were lots of volunteers. At my little brother's tournaments, I had to work in the canteen.

"When I found out how easy it was to do this through the NHLPA, I started wondering why everybody didn't do it. For me it's a way to pay back the community where I got started. We have a couple of big-name guys from Saskatchewan, but for me it seems like we have the muck-and-grind type of guys, the guys who play a hard game. We're proud of that. We're proud that Saskatchewan produces those types of players and those types of guys. A lot of the Saskatchewan guys I know are involved in charity events, involved in their communities, wherever they might be, at home or in the cities they're playing in."

The players, indeed, get involved in the communities where they play. Curtis Glencross of Kindersley appears regularly at Special Olympics functions. Cory Sarich of Davidson, a teammate of Glencross' in Calgary before being traded to Colorado in the summer of 2013, served as honourary chair of a golf tournament which raised funds for the Flames Foundation for Life and Children's Link Society.

It's common for NHL alumni to appear at charity events across Canada, and indeed many active players did so for things like the Hurricane Sandy Relief Fund during the most recent lockout. There are more specific contributions from players like Regina-born Anaheim Ducks captain Ryan Getzlaf, whose Getzlaf Golf Shootout raises money to fight Duchenne's Muscular Dystrophy. Laurie Boschman, born in Kerrobert, played 14 years in the NHL, became part of Christian Ministries International and conducts tournaments across Canada for Hockey Helps the Homeless. While with the Toronto Maple Leafs, Saskatoon's Luke Schenn established "Luke's Troops" to award game tickets to members of the Canadian Forces, plus he participated in the Team Up Foundation to help give Toronto kids a place to play and he served as an ambassador for Easter Seals. Every NHL team gets immersed in charity work throughout its community — in St. Louis the program is called the "14 Fund" after Regina's Doug Wickenheiser, a Blues alumnus who died of cancer in 1999. According to the team, The Blues 14 Fund has contributed $2.5 million "to positively impact programs and services that improve the health and wellness of youth in the St. Louis Area." Hall of Famer Gordie Howe is involved with the Alzheimer's Society, an organization that stages fund-raising games that readily attract NHL alumni. The Detroit Red Wings players have put pink tape on their sticks to show their support in the fight against breast cancer. Like numerous NHL players, Wawota-born Washington Capitals forward Brooks Laich is personally involved with Flashes of Hope, part of Hockey Fights Cancer, a project that gets children with life-threatening illnesses together for photographs with pro athletes.

Neudorf's Jarret Stoll hosted a golf tournament in Saskatoon, which raised $1 million in six years for the Jarret Stoll Patient Comfort Fund Endowment for Children at Royal University Hospital. Luke and Brayden Schenn, Saskatoon natives and Philadelphia Flyers teammates, replaced Stoll on the letterhead in 2012. Jordan Eberle was easily convinced by the Hospitals of Regina Foundation to help with the "Jordan Eberle and Friends Golf Tournament." He brought along teammates Ryan Nugent-Hopkins and Devan Dubnyk, Washington defenceman Mike Green, Carolina Hurricanes forward Zach Boychuk and Columbus Blue Jackets draft pick Ryan Murray. The second annual event sold out months in advance.

Keith Aulie, whose home town of Rouleau served as the fictional town of Dog River for the TV comedy series "Corner Gas" that was invented by another Saskatchewan native, Brent Butt, has also gotten involved in a fund-raising golf tournament.

"Mostly it's Saskatchewan guys who know about Dog River, where it is, and they've seen the ("Corner Gas") show on TV," said Aulie. "I hear a little bit when people ask where I'm from, I tell them about it. I call it Rouleau, I only call it Dog River to make a joke. I'm from Rouleau. Most of us don't come from big corporation families, or rich families. I don't want to make it a stereotype, but it seems like a lot of the Saskatchewan players are from rural families, from hard-working families, it's just kind of born into us and it shows through in a lot of our games. I'm not taking anything away from guys from different places, but I think we're kind of known for that. I try to keep that end of the bargain every time I go onto the ice."

A product of the WHL's Brandon Wheat Kings, Aulie was drafted by Calgary and subsequently traded to Toronto and Tampa Bay. Aulie's name, plus those of some NHL cohorts, highlights the tournament dubbed Hockey and Hearts. It's designed to raise money for local projects, specifically upgrading Rouleau's rink and attached curling club.

"In the summertime everyone's rushing in all directions, but in the winter you need someplace to gather, whether it's the curling rink for a fun bonspiel or steak nights, which we try to have every second Friday," said Bill Aulie, Keith Aulie's father and long-time Rouleau resident. "We have one spot, the rink, which is a good place to gather. Some of the young parents are on their own every night, so they can come over and have the chance to see everybody.

"We had a key to the rink, but other people would borrow it, they would clean the ice — it takes a whole community. Families would take a shift, take a whole week to volunteer and work the booths. It's nice to give back. Although we don't have any kids at the rink anymore, hopefully we can have an environment at the rink that lets some kids enjoy their time at the rink as much as Keith did."

The funds raised through Aulie's golf tournament — helped by a $50,000 government grant — paid to upgrade the rink's kitchen, concession and lobby areas, improve the dressing rooms and make the facility more accessible for wheelchairs and the elderly. Other special projects also receive funding, including the Mandi Schwartz Foundation, named after a 23-year-old hockey player at Yale who died of cancer in 2011. She was the older sister of Jaden and Rylan Schwartz, who lived in Wilcox, attended Athol Murray College of Notre Dame, advanced to Colorado College and aspire to great NHL careers — Jaden with the Blues (St. Louis drafted him 14th overall in 2010) and Rylan with the San Jose Sharks, who signed him as an undrafted free agent in April, 2013.

"People in Saskatchewan are awesome," Jaden Schwartz said before teeing off in the tournament. "You have so many friends here, your family, these guys — you always want to come back. Things like this you want to be a part of, it's a great thing. Everybody seems to come home for the summer to see their family and friends. A golf tournament is an easy thing to give back with. It's a great thing, it's for charity. When you know Aulie, the Schenns, you want to help out."

Most of the Hockey and Hearts tournament's legwork is done by Bill Aulie, whose farm sits kitty-corner to Rouleau. With help from a volunteer committee, he gets sponsors, books the course, arranges transportation and the banquet and promotes the event. Keith entices his hockey-playing friends and teammates to participate. One of the celebrities in the tournament was Mark McMorris, an X-Games snowboarder from Regina who donated a personalized snowboard for auction. It was alongside a Flyers jersey autographed by Claude Giroux, an Oilers jersey autographed by

Jordan Eberle and a potpourri of hockey memorabilia. McMorris' board went first in the auction, for $1,500, sold to Toronto Maple Leafs forward Tyler Bozak, who was also playing in the event. There are no golf courses in Rouleau, so buses and motorhomes hauled participants from the community hall to Moose Jaw and back. A local chef catered the banquet upon the golfers' return.

"We grossed $125,000," said Bill Aulie. "Number 1 was raising money for the rink. Mandi Schwartz was a good friend of Keith's; they've named a bursary after her at Notre Dame, so we figured it was a natural thing to put some money into Mandi's bursary at Notre Dame. If not for Notre Dame, Keith wouldn't be where he is. He played there a bit and they were very good to him; they open their doors for him to work out in the summertime. It's a nice way to give back to Notre Dame and a nice thing for Mandi and her family. As some of the dollars have started to grow, I've promoted that we're going to be sort of an umbrella group for our community. The rink will be our primary beneficiary and Mandi Schwartz is high on our priorities, but we had a boy this year — a grandson of a local farmer — who needed our help and we wanted to give some money to them. I have higher aspirations of raising more money for other things: Our dance club is struggling in town, the ball diamonds need some upgrading, the tennis courts/ outdoor summer hockey rink need some money. For all that stuff, Hockey and Hearts can be a beneficiary for them. We had some expenses but we still made $88,000 — with the $50,000 grant that's $138,000."

On Aulie's farm they grow durham and canola, two of the more common seed grains in Saskatchewan. In an adjoining pasture Bill Aulie raises Clydesdale horses. He's not a breeder; he buys the horses and trains them. Aulie's herd ranges in number from 18 to 50 and "about 10" of them throughout the years have been bought by Budweiser, the American beer company that prominently advertises its wagon-pulling Clydesdales. Bill's son prefers farming.

"From a young age I always loved the farm, being out there with the crops," said Keith Aulie. "I love the challenges you face farming, mostly to do with the weather. It's exciting and something to keep my mind off hockey. After focusing on hockey all winter it's nice to get out on the open prairies, spend some time on the farm, going in a different direction, and it's nice to spend some time with the family. Farming has come a long way, it's so much more of a science now, using technology. I like that stuff. Dad and I complement each other — he's good with the mechanical stuff and I'm good with the technological side of things, using computers to figure things out. We work well together. That's the plan right now (to farm), but you can never look too far into the future. I don't know if I'll ever want to be anything different; I just love the summers spent farming and coming home. I guess when you look into the future and have a dream, maybe you want to do that."

On one trip home, Keith Aulie repaid his community and his father in a way nobody could ever have imagined. Keith was playing in a hockey tournament in Regina during the Christmas holiday, so he was able to stay at home for a few nights and take part in an Aulie family tradition — a Christmas-time skate on one of the farm's dugouts, basically a slough that would freeze over.

"It was the 23rd of December," said Keith Aulie. "We were

cleaning snow off the dugout. (Bill) took off in his tractor, got about three-quarters of the way across and 'Bam!' He went straight down to the bottom. I was on the other end and ran straight over. The dugout was a little smaller than a hockey rink. There was a glass cab on the tractor. He went straight through the ice, but the tractor plugged most of the hole. After a couple of seconds the back window shattered and he ended up swimming out. He had about 40 pounds of gear on in the middle of winter.

"The scariest part was when he was flailing around at the bottom of the ice. I could see him through the ice. He started going the wrong way! I wondered what I was going to do because the tractor was plugging the hole, so there was hardly any room for him to get out. I don't know what it was, but he started coming back the other way and kind of got his arm out. I reached down, got a hold of him, and started pulling him out. The weirdest thing I think about was, before he got on the tractor to go out, he said, 'Would you watch, see what the ice is like with me?' It was 6 o'clock, supper time, we had just finished feeding the horses. At supper time you like to go in, get warmed up, having something to eat. I could wait for that, but for some reason I said, 'Yes.' Ninety per cent of the time I would usually say, 'No.' It's a good thing I was there."

Outstanding defenceman Nick Schultz played minor hockey in Strasbourg before going to play with Prince Albert in the WHL.

SASKATCHEWAN'S SUPPORT SYSTEMS

I t might be only a slight exaggeration to say that everyone who lives in Saskatchewan knows an NHLer. Maybe it's a former player, or maybe a current player was a teammate of your son in minor hockey or maybe you're the second cousin of Chris Kunitz, Brenden Morrow or Wade Redden. It's a tight-knit province and there are ties that keep pro hockey players in the hearts and minds of the people of Saskatchewan.

When four Saskatchewan-connected NHLers died in a space of a few months in 2010, the province's hockey community was left reeling. The string of tragedies began with the death of Derek Boogaard, who was born in Saskatoon and grew up in Regina. An NHL enforcer, Boogaard played five seasons with the Minnesota Wild and one with the New York Rangers before accidentally consuming a lethal mix of alcohol and drugs.

Shortly after this blow came news of the deaths of two recently retired NHLers, Wade Belak and Rick Rypien. Belak, a native of Saskatoon who grew up in North Battleford, played for the junior Blades and later for four NHL teams in 12 seasons before retiring in 2010. Rypien was an Alberta native, but he had been a popular captain of the WHL's Regina Pats before a pro career in which he bounced between the Vancouver Canucks and American Hockey League's Manitoba Moose. Reports said Belak and Rypien suffered from depression, which led to suicide.

In early September 2011, the entire hockey world was stunned by the tragic plane crash that killed every member of the Lokomotiv Yaroslavl team of Russia's Kontinental Hockey League. The team's head coach was Brad McCrimmon, a native of Plenty, Saskatchewan. McCrimmon played junior hockey with the Brandon Wheat Kings, and professionally with six teams during a distinguished 18-year NHL career. He later coached the WHL's Saskatoon Blades from 1998–2000 and served as an assistant coach at the NHL level. He was starting his first job as head coach of a professional team when the chartered Russian jet crashed while en route to its season-opening game.

One of those deeply saddened by McCrimmon's death was Lorne Molleken, a former Chicago Blackhawks head coach who grew up in Regina and was the Blades' head coach and general manager at the time of the crash.

"I really got to know Brad years ago when we taught hockey schools in Swift Current for a number of summers — the Stan Dunn/Ron Munro Hockey School," said Molleken. "It's unbelievable. Hard to believe. I can remember this summer when Brad stepped down in Detroit [as a Red Wings assistant coach] and everybody thought he was going to get a head job right away. Next thing you know he's on his way over to Russia."

"Saskatchewan kids are brought up knowing they have to work hard for everything and to do whatever's necessary to succeed," he added, "It's the Saskatchewan way."

Kelly McClintock, general manager of the Saskatchewan Hockey Association, knew McCrimmon and Rypien, plus he had family and hockey connections with Boogaard and Belak. That's how it works in Saskatchewan.

"This is a big province, a big area, with only a million people, but it's bound together by lots of things, including its hockey players," said McClintock. "When Beast [McCrimmon's nickname] was coaching the Blades he would phone me at lunch. 'Kel, what are you doing? Let's talk hockey.' So we'd shoot the shit for an hour or so. He wouldn't just talk about the Blades. He would talk about the minor hockey program in Plenty, about the parents he was dealing with, about other hockey associations and the players he was watching around the province. NHL players they might have been, but they know the province. They know everybody."

Just as the hockey community of Saskatchewan remembers Brad McCrimmon, so did McCrimmon remember the individuals and organizations that fostered his career and are still supporting hockey players. One such organization is the Saskatchewan Hockey Association. The SHA oversees all of the province's amateur hockey. It has a 274-page handbook posted on-line that details insurance policies, age restrictions and categories, discipline and appeal procedures, playing regulations, and provides information for coaches, officials and players. The SHA doesn't brag about producing NHL players, mainly because the vast majority of its members will advance no further than playing minor hockey.

Only the elite talents make it to the pinnacle of the hockey world.

"In minor hockey we're at about 23,000 (registrants), with 3,600 senior players," said Kelly McClintock. "That's more than anyone else in the country for senior hockey. Lots of provinces have rec(reational) hockey, but for senior, contact hockey we're clearly the biggest. It's the culture. If you go into places like Strasbourg, even now, kids want to play for their home towns. They grow up watching the senior teams and want to play there. If a town doesn't have a senior team, or it leaves, there's a void in the community. On Friday nights or Saturday nights, it's the gathering place. It's a huge part of the culture.

"Nick Schultz, when he was in Minnesota, had a fund-raiser that paid for a trip to a (Wild) game, the airfare, got a sponsor, gave them a tour of the dressing room and he had dinner with them," said McClintock. "I see (former NHLer) Sheldon Kennedy quite a bit, talking about Maryfield and Elkhorn, he remembers that along the border. We had Hockey Day in Canada in Carlyle — Brenden Morrow and Jim McKenzie were there. They're just regular guys. You couldn't really pick them out.

"When they had that rink improvement (program to help small towns upgrade their hockey facilities), there was more money given to rinks in Saskatchewan than anywhere else. All of a sudden, Spyhill's rink has Plexiglas? Jeff Odgers, what are you doing? Manor gets Plexiglas. Nobody's skating in Manor. Dean Kennedy's down there, he helped with the application. So all these places were getting Plexiglas and Zambonis and uniforms."

Tiger Williams, the NHL's all-time penalty leader, said his NHL career was a tribute to the people who supported him while he was growing up; judging by how Williams and his peers give back to their communities and show their appreciation for the support, that's a common sentiment.

Likewise, the people of the province take pride in the accomplishments of the kids who grew up and played at least some of their minor hockey in Saskatchewan. There were fellow townspeople who flooded the ice and scraped it between periods of early morning games during winter weekends, they flipped hamburgers in the concession stands, coached the minor hockey teams or sold Loonie sticks as a fund-raiser. Loonie sticks are hockey sticks with dollar-coins taped to them; people buy lottery tickets and the owner of the winning ticket takes home the Loonie stick.

There were also billets who looked after you when you were 16 years old and away from home, playing hockey, for the first time in your life. There were the parents of teammates who, when your parents were busy, drove you to your team's games or practices and brought you safely home. And there were your parents, who probably taught you to skate, perhaps flooded a backyard rink, bought your equipment, woke you up, fed you and — with a coffee mug perched on their van's steering wheel — drove you across the city to the rink for workouts, or across Western Canada to attend tournaments.

"I went through an Astro van every three years," said Darren Eberle, father of Regina-born Edmonton Oilers forward Jordan Eberle, reminiscing about the days spent travelling with his wife Lisa, Jordan and their other children, Dustin, Whitney and Ashley. "I'd start out with a new van, three years later Lisa would get that one and we'd sell the other one. I remember one year we didn't sell it — we literally had three vans sitting in the driveway. In Saskatchewan, we went to a whole lot of places. With Jordan it was a little different. Right after that Super Novice tournament in Edmonton, we went with a team called the Boston Icemen to Toronto. Then we went to Quebec. Detroit one time. Went to Boston. That was kind of neat for a couple years, where they actually flew us out there, the kids and Lisa and me. It was a family holiday. This guy had deep pockets and he was financing it all, with some Canadian kids on his team. We ended up playing with Steve Stamkos, Travis Hamonic, when they were added to the team. We know the Stamkos family quite well. We were with (the elite, summer travelling team) Saskatchewan Wheatland. We went to the Brick tournament with a Vancouver team. We know the Schwartz family (of Wilcox), closer to home. Dustin and Whitney played with and against the Schwartz family, on summer teams. Dustin was on Saskatchewan Wheatland, too. Whitney played hockey, Ashley was in gymnastics. Those were our holidays. We spent a lot of money for all our kids, but we never really thought about that. We knew we were spending money, but I kind of justified it based on, 'This is going to be our holidays.' And we kind of enjoyed it."

Saskatchewan's top hockey products are, of course, similar to elite players from every province or country. They all love the game and spent every possible moment skating, practising, playing shinny or some version of the sport. They dreamed about playing in the NHL and worked toward their goal, but for the most part retained their humility when they advanced to the top level.

"Their mentality seems to be different," said Lisa Eberle.

"They're a little more humble because that's not where they expect they're going to be. They work hard to get there.

"I never had to drag Jordan to the rink. Was he waiting for me to go? I'm not going to say all the time, but probably the majority of the time, probably 90 per cent of the time it was like that. When he was younger it was sometimes a little harder, but he never didn't want to go to the rink. It's not like he ever thought it was too much. When he was younger we had him doing other things as well. He liked baseball, so he played it. He worked at it. He went to bed early when he had a game the next morning. He tried to eat the right things. It's funny even now, if he doesn't get his training in he's feeling guilty."

Every player interviewed for this book, when asked to explain how he made it to the National Hockey League, gave credit to his parents. In a more modern fashion, Wawota's Brook Laich pays homage to his parents, brother and sister in one part of his on-line blog and website, which also shows pictures of him playing for the Washington Capitals. The NHLers also cite coaches, unpaid volunteers, teammates and mentors for providing the advice and support that helped them along the way. Quite a few of them, including Eberle, had a career stop at Wilcox, a town about 50 kilometres south of Regina and home of Athol Murray College of Notre Dame. Among the noteworthy NHL players who attended Notre Dame are: Wendel Clark, Curtis Joseph, Brad Richards, Vincent Lecavalier, Keith Aulie and Jaden Schwartz. The college was established in the 1920s and '30s by "Pere" Athol Murray, a Hockey Hall of Fame member. The school's motto is "Struggle and Emerge." In the early days, according to movies and books and Murray's own words, it was a struggle to keep the school alive, but it always seemed capable of icing hockey teams. It has progressed to the point where the college now supports nine male teams and three female teams, from bantam to junior, and attracts prospects from across the country and helps turn them into top-notch players.

"It's a Prairie thing," said Rob Palmarin, the school's president. "Wendel (Clark) was there last week, his son's in Grade 8, and he was there for a hockey school. Whatever it is: Play pro then go home and help on the farm, that unselfish mentality.

"I think we're a key part of Saskatchewan. We're developing players at the minor-hockey level, the bantam and midget and junior. We help develop not only the skills, but the character. We teach our guys to expect the adversity, expect to face the difficulties and what are you going to do? That was totally Father Murray. All these guys grow up with that. They have that willingness to go to the hockey rink every day. The temptation for today's kid is PlayStation. If they want to play now they have to go to the weight room and the rink."

The graduates never forget their roots. They give back to the school in various forms, often by donations or simply by paying it homage during their careers, which leads more players through the doors. In Saskatchewan, it's customary to remember where you came from.

Nick Schultz, a defenceman from Strasbourg who was traded in 2012 from the Minnesota Wild to Edmonton, found a wonderful way to commemorate his late father, Robert, for all the work his dad put into the town's rink.

"Robert was a caretaker at the rink, he drove the Zamboni, he coached. He would leave the shop after working all day and go to the rink to coach," said Nick's mother, Carol Schultz, who recently concluded 28 years serving on town council with an eight-year term as mayor of Strasbourg.

"Nick and his brothers (Kris and Terrance) were at the rink all the time," remembered Carol. "They watched all those guys, all the senior teams. Robert's cousins, Clayton and Warren, were with the (senior) Maroons. And Uncle John was involved in the hockey here.

"We had three boys playing. If Robert wasn't coaching one of them, he was coaching two of them. Nick played a little with Terrance, our second son; they brought Nick up even though he was three years younger. I can't imagine how many games we've watched. The rink opened in '82. It's not like we had access to the rink but every time they could get on the rink for public skating, they were there. They loved being out there with all their friends. If they weren't at the rink they were outside on our streets playing shinny. Terrance was a goalie, so he got lots of workouts."

About a decade ago the Schultz family began a four-on-four tournament that traditionally ended the hockey season in Strasbourg. The tournament was just one of a number of fund-raisers Nick Schultz got involved with that helped put Plexiglas around the rink and provided, through the NHLPA's Goals and Dreams program, 75 uniforms to minor hockey teams in Strasbourg.

"The year Robert passed away (2008)," said Carol Schultz, "when they did the Schultz four-on-four, all the memorial money went to buy a new Zamboni for our rink. It wasn't a brand-new one, it was a couple years old, and they put on the side of it a cross with Robert's initials on it. The memorial money was quite a bit; Nick topped it up."

When Brett Clark needed advice as an aspiring hockey player, the soon-to-be NHLer could ask his mother's brother for advice — Dave Dunn, Clark's uncle, was from the same home town of Wapella. Dunn played minor hockey and senior hockey during the same season before attending the University of Saskatchewan, where he played varsity hockey for four years. Unscouted and undrafted, Dunn asked the expansion Vancouver Canucks for a tryout in 1970, which led to him playing three seasons in the minors before joining the NHL team. One game into his second season with Vancouver, 1974–75, Dunn got traded to the Toronto Maple Leafs. He spent two campaigns in Toronto before capping his career with a two-year stint with the World Hockey Association's Winnipeg Jets, who won the WHA's final championship in 1978.

"Maybe, for some reason we succeed because we watch the (Saskatchewan) Roughriders," Dunn said. "We're not supposed to win, we're a small town, the smallest (Canadian Football League) centre, yet we're still the Number One franchise because of its fan support. Everybody cheers for us. When I came out of college, I hadn't played a game of junior. Dick Irvin (Jr., the Hall of Fame broadcaster who grew up in Regina) told me when we were in Montreal playing the Canadiens, he came into the dressing room afterwards and said, 'Dave, I just want to welcome you aboard. I'm an alumnus from the (University of Saskatchewan). I followed your career with interest because you're the only kid I know of right now who never played a game of junior and is right now playing in the NHL.' There were lots of kids who played junior, then went to college, but I didn't even play a junior A game. I played midget hockey for the Wapella Blackhawks; I was old enough to play midget and good enough to play senior, so I played them both. Then I made the Huskies, played there four years, then wrote a letter to see if I could get into the Vancouver Canucks' expansion camp. I wrote a letter and they wrote back that if I made the team they would reimburse my expenses. I went to their camp and made the farm team. That's the Saskatchewan way."

Dunn, a successful businessman in the Regina area, has happily watched his nephew progress from his minor hockey days in Wapella and Whitewood, to the SJHL's Melville Millionaires and the University of Maine Black Bears in 1995–96, followed by a stint with the Canadian national team and 17 seasons with 10 different pro teams.

"Brett was trying to decide where to go out of Melville on a scholarship," said Dunn. "His dad and I met with some of the recruiters from Maine and the various other colleges that wanted him. He asked me what I thought. I told him I didn't know American colleges but I thought it was the right move for him. I can't remember the other colleges, but the coach from Maine spoke to us in my living room. He flew up, we met in the living room and had a nice talk. That worked out well.

"I don't know how far skill can take you. I told (Clark's late agent) Don Baizley many times that nobody knows how good this kid is until you go and watch him. Andy Murray, who coached Brett with the national team, said he's the best practice player ever because he worked hard on every drill. He never gives the puck away. He's not scared at all; you can't have any fear in your body and be successful at that level. He's kind of got a Wayne Gretzky trait: He thinks the game a step ahead. All of his passes are to where the players are going to be. He just has that instinct. I'm surprised he's played so many years, not because he didn't have the ability. I knew that. Physically he's not big, but again he has that Gretzky skill: How to stay out of traffic and roll with the checks. He's had a couple fairly serious injuries, but playing 13 years in the NHL! It's been a great career for him."

Dunn recalled that when he was growing up, Wapella had a flourishing minor hockey system. Unfortunately there are so few kids left in Wapella and other towns, some of the smaller centres have either given up their hockey programs or combined them with other towns or villages. All minor hockey programs are under the jurisdiction of the SHA, with the two biggest organizations obviously located in the province's biggest cities, Saskatoon and Regina. Each oversees about 2,500 boys and girls.

Hockey Regina, the SHA and Saskatoon Minor Hockey Association are volunteer-run operations, for the most part, with paid employees on staff to deal with the day-to-day issues such as uniform distribution, scheduling games and practices, paying officials, plus collecting registrations and the appropriate fees while making sure the regulations are properly followed. Sometimes players advance to the NHL, which is a source of pride and inspiration within each association. But it's not the reason why they exist.

"We had three (Saskatoon products) debut within a week or

so (in the 2013 NHL season)," said Kelly Boes, executive director of the Saskatoon Minor Hockey Association. "Darcy Kuemper got his first game in with the Minnesota Wild, Sean Collins with Columbus and Eric Gryba stayed with Ottawa right into the playoffs. Eric came right through our association, played (AAA midget) for the Contacts. Darcy played til he was 17, didn't even leave for major junior until he was 18. There's another example that if you don't make it at 16 or 17 at the highest level you can still make it. Sean Collins didn't really do anything until he was 18, a late bloomer until he got into junior A and got a scholarship. Next thing you know he's getting signed right out of college, just like Andrew Johnston, who got signed out of Humboldt last year and signed with the (Philadelphia) Flyers. He grew up playing in the Bobcats zone in Saskatoon, played a little Tier I and got himself a pretty good career in junior A and somebody noticed him. He wasn't good enough for major junior, goes back to junior A and ends up having a great year as a 20-year-old and ends up getting signed. He had a scholarship opportunity, too, but he ended up taking the three-year entry level deal and ran with it.

"It's one of those things that feeds itself: The more kids who see it, the more are inspired by it. In my position you try not to emphasize that kind of thing, that we're producing NHL players. But we can't emphasize that, even though they tend to be nice stories and almost to a man they've been great ambassadors for us. It says a lot about our culture here: Most of their parents would give them a whupping if they didn't help out. Most of these guys have a ton of time in the offseason so they come back to help us out."

Although Saskatchewan produces more NHL players per

capita than any other province, state or country, there's not always a common theory on the best way to produce them. Making the NHL takes talent, an incredible work ethic, dedication to the game, a few good breaks and, possibly, the advantage of playing in a system that best helps a young player develop. They may be comparable in size, but Regina and Saskatoon have differing philosophies on how best to develop each respective city's top players and, hand in hand, keep boys and girls interested in playing the game.

"A lot of kids and a lot of parents think they're going to be NHL prospects," said Blair Watson, executive director of Hockey Regina. "It's difficult sometimes. When they haven't seen the end product, when they've maybe only seen pee wee, they're saying, 'He can't miss!' We're saying, 'He's 12!' You always have to temper them because you're always going to have nutbars; unfortunately you can't get away from the nutbars. You try to temper them, but you try to let them know — their kids are 12! Even when they get to bantam, age 14, sometimes the best players aren't even playing yet. You keep the programs there so there's an opportunity for everyone to play at their skill level and their commitment level. You give them the opportunity, but for the most part it's God-given talent that determines how they move up the ladder. As they move up the ladders and up the tiers, that pie gets awfully small. You try to temper it and try to keep as many kids playing as possible. The more kids playing, the better your pool of talent."

Hockey Regina is an amalgamation of several different groups which ran minor hockey in the city for years — Regina Boys Community Hockey League, Queen City Minor Hockey

Association and City of Regina's Parks League were among the predecessors. Regina's earliest NHL products advanced strictly through the system set up by the junior Pats. Because Hockey Regina, per se, has been around for only 12 years, Eberle is one of the first NHL products whose entire minor hockey career was under the auspices of Hockey Regina.

Northwest on Highway 11 about 250 kilometres, the Saskatoon Minor Hockey Association could boast about recent grads Luke and Brayden Schenn, James Wright and Carter Ashton. The cities seem to take turns pouring out batches of NHLers and, quietly, the SMHA is just as proud of its other products.

"It's the philosophy of Saskatoon minor hockey to get as many kids playing at a high level as possible, especially at the younger ages," said Boes. "We've had a different philosophy from Hockey Regina. It's still our intention to do that as much as possible. The higher-line parents want to cut down as much as possible because that third line just isn't good enough. Some coaches think their third line isn't good enough either. It's been helpful giving kids more chances to play at a higher level. The longer they can hang in there playing a higher level, the longer they continue playing, there's less of a dropout rate and they keep striving to play at that level.

"There are so many good stories of kids who played the top level of hockey until midget or so; maybe they didn't make the NHL but they maybe moved on to play junior or get scholarships. There's a '91-born kid, his name is Coltyn Sanderson. It's such a neat story: He played one year of Tier I hockey in his whole career, that was when he was 17, and he went on to try out for the

(SJHL's) Weyburn Red Wings at 18. He got cut. He was going to come home, maybe go to work and play Junior B in Saskatoon. Instead he took the advice of somebody from Weyburn who suggested he play for the Junior B team in Assiniboia. They said they had a good connection with Weyburn and they would stay in touch. Instead of just quitting, he played there, ended up playing two years in Weyburn and became their captain before going to UND (University of North Dakota) on a full scholarship. A great story about never giving up. We keep seeing that."

Foam Lake's Bernie Federko had four 100 point seasons and eight seasons where he scored more than 90 points.

A HALL OF
OUR OWN

Bernie Federko's hockey career is memorialized inside the Hockey Hall of Fame, a beautiful shrine located in a stately former bank building in downtown Toronto. Long before his 2002 induction into the Hall, Federko's achievements were well-known and proudly displayed in Foam Lake, Saskatchewan. Drive along Highway 16, the northerly Trans-Canada Highway known as the Yellowhead because of its eventual path through the Rocky Mountains, and about midway into the 1,100-kilometre drive between Lloydminster and Winnipeg is Federko's home town. At the entrance to the Foam Lake Golf & Country Club sits a wooden, one-storey building that serves as a clubhouse, a visitor's information booth and a place to register for overnight stays at the nearby campground. At one end of the gravel parking lot is a large billboard, adorned with a pink ribbon, which reads "Proud to be Home of the Breast Friends," a group of women — including breast-cancer survivors — from Foam Lake who have raised $1.4 million for cancer research through sales of their cookbooks.

At the other end of the parking lot are laudatory posters of four hockey players and a sign that reads "Foam Lake Hockey Heroes: Dedicated in recognition of the individuals from this community who have achieved national and international stature in professional hockey."

It's a traditional practice across Western Canada for cities, towns and villages to honour their sports heroes with signage: In Langenburg, just down the Yellowhead from Foam Lake, former Edmonton Oilers captain Kelly Buchberger has a sign, though it's less conspicuous than the sign commending his sister Kerri, a long-time member of the Canadian women's volleyball team. In Foxwarren, Manitoba, they have signs feting home-town NHLers Pat Falloon, Ron Low and Mark Wotton. Also on the Yellowhead is Saltcoats, which hasn't produced an NHL player but is sign-worthy proud of world-champion curlers Joan (Inglis) McCusker and Steve Laycock.

Foam Lake's Hockey Heroes display celebrates the careers of Pat Elynuik, Ted Hargreaves, Dennis Polonich and Bernie Federko. Elynuik won the 1985 Memorial Cup with the WHL's Prince Albert Raiders, was a first-round draft choice of the Winnipeg Jet, played 506 regular-season games and earned 342 points with four NHL teams — Winnipeg, Washington, Tampa Bay and Ottawa — before retiring in 1997. Hargreaves won a bronze medal with Canada's hockey team at the 1968 Olympics and played one season with the World Hockey Association's Jets, but never appeared in the NHL. Polonich, an eighth-round draft choice by Detroit in 1973, played junior for the WCHL's Flin Flon Bombers and eventually played 390 regular-season games, earning 1,242 penalty minutes, with the Red Wings. Federko is the biggest star of the four Foam Lake honorees.

In 1975–76, his third and final year of junior hockey, Bernie Federko amassed 72 goals and 115 assists in 72 games with the Saskatoon Blades, giving him 344 points in 206 WCHL games. Federko was drafted seventh overall by the St. Louis Blues, began his pro career in the minors, but got summoned to The Show during his first season out of junior. He evolved into such an offensive talent that three seasons later he recorded 95 points for St. Louis. He eventually tallied 1,130 points on 369 goals and 761 assists in 1,000 NHL games over the course of 13 seasons in St. Louis and a final campaign, 1989–90, with Detroit. A shifty centre capable of making his teammates better, Federko's notoriety suffered because the Blues never advanced further than the semifinals, coming closest to a Stanley Cup finals appearance with a seventh-game, 2–1 loss against the Calgary Flames in a 1986 divisional final. He was often described as one of the league's most under-rated players. He was not under-rated in St. Louis, however. Less than a year after he retired, the Blues retired Federko's sweater number 24; 10 years later he was voted into the Hockey Hall of Fame. But no matter how far you go, when you're a Saskatchewan kid you remember the early days.

"We had a great building in Foam Lake; the rink was right across the street from us," Federko said via telephone from St. Louis in October, 2012. "When I was six or seven years old, it burned down. That was a sad day, and I remember people with their hoses out, hosing down our house across the street so it wouldn't burn. It took two or three years to build another rink, a nice one with a curling rink. It was seven or eight blocks away, in town. In the meantime, Dad flooded the garden every year. There weren't a lot of ponds or sloughs around, not around the Foam Lake area. Dad would put two-by-fours around the garden. We'd shovel the snow. By the end of the winter we would have snow piled about eight feet tall! It would be great because the pucks never left the yard. We would find some pucks every spring after the snow melted. We'd take the hose out and re-flood it when the ice got roughed up. We'd spend hours and hours out there. The yards weren't really that big. We'd play under the light from the back of the house, me and my three brothers. A lot of the boys in town were closer to my older brothers' age. At my age there were more girls than boys, so I actually played more with my brothers' friends than my friends, even though they were all spread out and not close to our house in our little town.

"We played street hockey. If we weren't in the backyard we were out on the street, putting chunks of snow or stones to mark the goals. We played on grid roads, but there was so much snow, they didn't grade it off, cars drove over it. We had streetlights — one was one house down and the other was the other way, one house down. It was so shiny we could have played all night long if we were on the road because the streetlights were so bright. The puck would slide really well because the road was smooth from all the cars going over it. It was like ice."

Federko had just visited Saskatchewan before this conversation took place. He had gone to Saskatoon to see his family and friends, so the Blades piggy-backed his visit into a promotional tour to remind hockey fans that the 2013 Memorial Cup, the championship of the 60 major junior hockey teams in Canada and the U.S., where eight of the franchises are located, was being played in Saskatatoon's Credit Union Centre. As the host team, the Blades were granted an automatic berth in the tournament along with the winners of the Western Hockey League, Ontario Hockey League and Quebec Major Junior Hockey League.

Although Federko settled with his family in St. Louis after his playing career and didn't return to Saskatchewan too often, he found himself staying in touch with his home province through his television job as a hockey analyst for Blues games.

"I think it's somewhat of a fraternity — I still follow the guys from Saskatchewan and the guys who played for the Blades," said Federko. "When somebody comes through here the first thing I look at when I'm looking through the rosters is, Where are they from or where did they play junior? If somebody comes from the same place as you, especially if it's Saskatchewan, it's a great place to grow up, so the roots we have in Saskatchewan and the way we're brought up, from Elmer Lach to all of us, are real. We're brought up in families that are real, who care about each other. We're all honest about where we're trying to go. We all look at Saskatchewan as being a big part of our lives.

"You start with something, you get an opportunity and you get the benefit of the doubt because you're working your tail off. If you make it, the people of Saskatchewan are very happy that you did make it.

"It's been a long time. I've been away for 36 years now. My mom's in Saskatoon, my dad passed away in January after 92 great years. He got pneumonia and couldn't fight through it;

it was very short. I was up to see him in early January because he wasn't feeling very well. It was nice to be there. My wife's mom is there. We're all really close families. I also saw some guys I hadn't seen for a long time. We still get back there once in awhile, but our family's lifestyles keep us here for most of the time. It's still home. (St. Louis) is home for us now; our children were born and raised here. But our home is still Saskatchewan. I don't get to Foam Lake very often because mom and dad moved out of there about 25 years ago. It's still where I got my start."

Federko was invited back to his home province to attend induction ceremonies in the summer of 2013 for the Saskatchewan Hockey Hall of Fame. He was part of the class which also included Clark Gillies of Moose Jaw, who won four Stanley Cups with the New York Islanders, Gordon "Red" Berenson of Regina, who played for the Regina Pats and University of Michigan before embarking on a 17-year NHL career and returning to coach at Michigan, and Eddie Shore, who was born in Fort Qu'Appelle and grew up on a farm near Cupar, known as "Old Blood and Guts" for the ferocity that helped him win the 1929 and 1939 Stanley Cups with Boston and be named the NHL's most valuable player four times during a 14-year NHL career.

The builders inducted in 2013 were Del Wilson of Regina, a former owner and general manager of the Pats who helped form the Western Canada Junior Hockey League, and Bill Hay of Saskatoon, who played for the Pats and Colorado College en route to an NHL career in which he won the Calder Trophy as the league's top rookie in 1960 and the next year's Stanley Cup with Chicago. Hay later served as president of Hockey Canada and the Calgary Flames before becoming chairman of the Hockey Hall of Fame, a role he relinquished in 2013. John Maddia of Indian Head, a former president of the Saskatchewan Amateur Hockey Association, was inducted as a grassroots builder and Mick McGeough of Regina, who worked more than 1,000 NHL games as a referee, was inducted as an official. The lone team inducted was the 1914 Regina Victorias, who won the Allan Cup as Canada's top senior team in their first year of existence.

It's really quite a remarkable group of inductees for such a small province. And think about this — this was the second group of inductees! Shore, Federko and Gillies are in the Hockey Hall of Fame. Shore is in the Canadian Hall of Fame. For logistical and a few other reasons, they waited a year for their enshrinement because the huge inaugural class of inductees was even more impressive: Hockey Hall of Famers Gordie Howe, Bryan Trottier, Sid Abel, Elmer Lach, Max and Doug Bentley, Johnny Bower, Glenn Hall and builders Athol Murray, Ed Chynoweth and Gordon Juckes. Other players inducted in 2012 were Fred Sasakamoose and Metro Pyrstai, who played 11 years in the NHL and won two Stanley Cups with Detroit. The other builders were Bill Hunter, former Calgary Flames co-owner Darryl "Doc" Scaman and grassroots organizer Bill Ford. Dennis Pottage, a former referee-in-chief for the Canadian Hockey Association, was the official. The inducted teams were the 1973–74 Regina Pats, 1984–85 Prince Albert Raiders, 1988–89 Swift Current Broncos — all Memorial Cup champions — plus the 1982–83 CIAU-winning University of Saskatchewan Huskies and an era of the Semans Wheat Kings that won five league championships and five provincial intermediate C crowns between 1955–64.

Before 2012 there was no special way of honouring Saskatchewan's hockey royalty. There is the Saskatchewan Sports Hall of Fame and Museum, which inducts hockey players, builders and teams as parts of its annual ceremonies and which has encouraged cities like Saskatoon, Regina and Prince Albert to establish their own Halls of Fame to honour home-town sports heroes. But despite the abundance of famous, talented and influential people from Saskatchewan scattered throughout the hockey world, the Saskatchewan Hockey Association had not established its own Hall of Fame until Marc Habscheid prompted it. Habscheid, a former NHL player who also coached Canada's national team and several junior teams, including the Kelowna Rockets when they won the Memorial Cup in 2004, started thinking that his province should set up its own shrine in Swift Current, his home town and a strong hockey community located on the Trans-Canada Highway on the route from Regina to Calgary.

"The funny thing about this is when I approached a few people about a Hall of Fame, there were some people interested but they didn't know each other," said Habscheid. "I said, 'Trust me; you'll all fit.' They did. And lots of people worked very hard to get it done."

The Saskatchewan Hockey Association jumped fully on board with the idea, supported by the Saskatchewan Sports Hall of Fame and Museum. SHA general manager Kelly McClintock helped assemble a board of directors and the committees necessary to run the Hall. Swift Current donated a site in its hockey arena, home of the WHL's Broncos, which was called the Civic Centre before being renamed the Credit Union iPlex. A room was set aside to house displays featuring jerseys, sticks, programs, testimonials and pictures of the inductees. When the Hall opened, even Marc Habscheid was impressed with what he learned about Saskatchewan's hockey history.

"There's a respect within the province for the game of hockey," said Habscheid. "It needed a Hockey Hall of Fame. This is so great to see...so much history involved and now it's coming to the forefront. I had no idea Johnny Bower and Elmer Lach were from Saskatchewan. To see people come back and what it means to them is spectacular. Right now Saskatchewan has about a million people; in years past there was even less. To have the impact that Gordie Howe or Glenn Hall or some of those builders have had, it's impressive for a province this size."

Saskatchewan's contribution to the NHL continues to be impressive. Quanthockey.com, perhaps the most current of the websites tracking Saskatchewan-born NHL players, showed 47 of them appeared in NHL games during the 2013, lockout-shortened NHL season — 11 from Saskatoon, 10 from Regina, 11 from other cities and 14 who were born in small towns, villages or rural settings. Knowing that three of the rural players were actually born in big cities, that means there were 17 current players who grew up in rural communities. Using those adjusted numbers, 64 per cent of the players from Saskatchewan in the NHL are from cities, which is a reflection of the province as a whole. According to the 2012 census, there were 1,072,082 residents of the province — 65 per cent is urban population and 35 per cent is rural population. They're all entwined, anyway. People from the cities depend on the farming economy, rural dwellers drop into the cities for entertainment and shopping. They know each other's business. It's a common refrain that everyone in Saskatchewan knows about the crops, the legislature and the Roughriders and everyone has an opinion about those topics. They also follow extremely closely the fortunes of the Saskatchewan kids in the NHL.

Among fans who follow the exploits of the new generation of NHLers are well-known former players like Orland Kurtenbach, who was inducted into the Saskatchewan Sorts Hall of Fame in 2012. When the NHL expanded into Vancouver in 1970, Kurtenbach became the team's first captain, an appropriate appointment considering that the Cudworth, Saskatchewan, native had played some semi-pro hockey in Vancouver between stints in the NHL.

As a kid Kurtenbach lived on a farm near Cudworth before moving with his family to Prince Albert, where he overcame early skating deficiencies, played junior hockey and was scouted by the New York Rangers. He had to work for everything he got.

"We moved off the farm and got there when I was 11 years old," said Kurtenbach. "I couldn't make a team because I couldn't skate. I had old skates; they looked like goalie skates. At that time, with the outdoor rinks, when you had a chance you would play and play and play. I caught up. In about four or five years, what really helped me was playing with the senior team that we had locally; it had some ex-juniors. That really helped me. The next year I played junior with the (Prince Albert) Mintos and was the rookie-of-the-year. That was really a big, big help to me. I was playing against grown men. They kicked the tar out of you. It wasn't dirty, but when you were fighting for the puck you were fighting against a grown man. You have no strength compared to them. I was 16. I went to the Rangers camp in Saskatoon. At that time there was a loose affiliation between the NHL and juniors. Flin Flon was sort of involved with the Rangers as well; they were able to pick me up for the Memorial Cup in 1956–57. I turned pro the next year with the Vancouver Canucks in the Western League. You had guys like Guyle Fielder, Phil Maloney. I went to the Buffalo Bisons (American Hockey League) the next year — there was Willie Marshall and Dunc Fisher. They weren't very big guys. But Guyle Fielder was the closest thing to a Wayne Gretzky in terms of handling the puck. I'm not too sure he wanted to be that type of player. From what I read he went up to Detroit and they put him with (Ted) Lindsay and (Gordie) Howe. There's no way — Gordie wanted the puck. I sort of felt the same way: I wanted the puck. Guyle's not going to have the puck when Gordie's there."

Kurtenbach went on to play 639 games in the NHL with the Rangers, Bruins, Leafs and finally the Canucks. Considered one of the best fighters of his era, Kurtenbach was also a productive forward. Upon joining the Canucks for their 1970–71 NHL debut, he tallied 53 points in 52 games and added 61, 28 and 21 points in three subsequent seasons before retiring. He had the opportunity to extend his career but declined an offer to join the World Hockey Association. Though he never played in the WHA, he appreciates what the upstart league did for players salaries.

"The NHL didn't market the way they do now. Our wages were shitty. They finally got it off the ground, but didn't really go until the World Hockey Association came in and Bobby

Hull signed with Winnipeg. I was fishing with Bobby and Andy Bathgate about 3–4 years ago on the West Coast. Bobby said, 'I would have stayed in Chicago for $600,000, but they wouldn't go for it.' I think he was making $400,000. (Blackhawks owner Bill) Wirtz wouldn't budge. Our wages didn't really start til about 1992–93. When we played in that old six-team league for those shitty wages it was a no-win situation other than playing for pride and the fact you made more money than the average person, but not a helluva lot more. When I was making minimum wage of $7,000 in Boston there were guys at home making $4,500 or $5,500."

One of the benefits of having a Hockey Hall of Fame in Saskatchewan is that it provides the occasion to bring hockey greats like Bernie Federko and Orland Kurtenbach together, to hear their take on the game of today and yesteryear and to have these and other keen observers discuss what makes Saskatchewan hockey players so special.

"I hate using the terms, but it's usually grit and heart, they just don't give up. It comes from the soil," Graham Tuer said with a laugh while attending the Hall's 2012 induction ceremonies in Regina. "We always had to make our own entertainment, so we went to the rink and spent hours and hours there. That was true up until 20 years ago."

For nearly half a century Graham Tuer has been scouting minor-hockey players for major junior teams and the SHA. He believes Saskatchewan players will long be in demand by NHL teams and the province is continuing to find ways to develop them.

"We're going to have fewer players because it costs so much.

It's a tremendous amount of money for a parent to lay out for a kid to play hockey. I worked this week at our Western Prospects camp — we had 150 kids there from British Columbia, Northwest Territories, Texas, Colorado, Manitoba and Saskatchewan. A good bunch of kids. Like everything else, when you put it on a distribution curve there are a few kids who really don't fit, but there are also some outstanding ones."

Tuer has certainly seen his share of prospects and players, including everyone in the group of Saskatchewan players who appeared in the NHL during the 2012–13 campaign. Here's that list from Quanthockey.com:

Patrick Marleau of Aneroid (San Jose), Brenden Morrow of Carlyle (Pittsburgh), Ryan Getzlaf of Regina (Anaheim), Scott Hartnell of Regina (Philadelphia), Wade Redden of Lloydminster (Boston), Chris Kunitz of Regina (Pittsburgh), Jarret Stoll of Melville (Los Angeles), Brooks Laich of Wawota (Washington), Curtis Glencross of Kindersley (Calgary), Colby Armstrong of Lloydminster (Montreal), Brett Clark of Wapella (Minnesota), Jordan Eberle of Regina (Edmonton), Blake Comeau of Meadow Lake (Columbus), Cory Sarich of Saskatoon (Calgary), Nick Schultz of Strasbourg (Edmonton), Tyler Bozak of Regina (Toronto), Boyd Gordon of Unity (Phoenix), Travis Moen of Swift Current (Montreal), Luke Schenn of Saskatoon (Philadelphia), Derek Dorsett of Kindersley (New York Rangers), Darroll Powe of Saskatoon (New York Rangers), Zack Smith of Maple Creek (Ottawa), Brayden Schenn of Saskatoon (Philadelphia), Darcy Hordichuk of Kamsack (Edmonton), Tanner Glass of Regina (Pittsburgh), Sheldon Brookbank of Lanigan (Chicago), Dwight

King of Meadow Lake (Los Angeles), Jared Cowen of Saskatoon (Ottawa), Jaden Schwartz of Melfort (St. Louis), Blair Jones of Central Butte (Calgary), Adam Cracknell of Prince Albert (St. Louis), Jordan Hendry of Nokomis (Anaheim), Brett Carson of Regina (Calgary), Tyson Strachan of Melfort (Florida), Keith Aulie of Rouleau (Tampa Bay), James Wright of Saskatoon (Winnipeg), Cam Ward of Saskatoon (Carolina), Brendan Mikkelson of Regina (Tampa Bay), Nolan Yonkman of Punnichy (Florida), Eric Gryba of Saskatoon (Ottawa), Dan Ellis of Saskatoon (Carolina), Steve MacIntyre of Brock (Pittsburgh), Braden Holtby of Lloydminster (Washington), Josh Harding of Regina (Minnesota), Devan Dubnyk of Regina (Edmonton), Darcy Kuemper of Saskatoon (Minnesota) and Sean Collins of Saskatoon (Columbus).

The players truly come from every corner of Saskatchewan, but it's not uncommon to have them bunched together, as Habscheid recalled from his days playing minor hockey.

"I grew up on a farm about 10 miles south of Swift Current," Habscheid said. "When I played bantam hockey in Swift Current, we had 15 players on the team. Years ago I counted after the fact that nine of them signed professional contracts. There was Rocky Trottier, Gord Kluzak, Lane Lambert, Mark Lamb, Stu Innes, Al Larochelle. It was incredible to see a small town produce that many players. At the time we were just a bunch of kids playing together, who didn't know what would happen. We didn't know any better. We played for the love of the game. Who's to say what would happen? I think it's the fact that for a lot of the kids, it was just a way of life. You lived and breathed it. It didn't matter if it was 50-below, if you found a puddle that had frozen over and was

10 yards around you'd get the skates and go and play. You played hockey because you loved it, it was our fibre, and we all understood it was such a privilege to be involved in the game."

Bryan Trottier's tiny home town of Val Marie sits in the southwest corner of Saskatchewan, close to Swift Current; the ranch he grew up on is about six miles from the Canada/U.S. border. Trottier recalls jokingly that his father's cattle would wander illegally into the U.S. on a daily basis.

"I have no clue why Saskatchewan produces so many hockey players," said Trottier, a winner of six Stanley Cups as a player — four with the New York Islanders and two with the Pittsburgh Penguins. But he does know, because he was one of them, one of the best. And he was speaking at festivities for the brand-new Saskatchewan Hockey Hall of Fame.

"It's something Saskatchewan should be proud of. Maybe it's the friendly, Prairie winters that allow us to have a lot of rinks and produce a lot of good players. There are lots of rinks per capita, a lot of ice for kids to get ice time. There's good coaching, good parents, good communities that support the hockey.

"Our little province has produced some great players and is rich in history at every level. All of our stories are a little different, but for all of us it's really hard, because if it was easy everybody would do it. It just makes a person appreciate it a little more. There are twists and turns and curves, but each one of us shares a common denominator: Our Saskatchewan roots."

CREDITS

Page 20: HHOF Images, Hockey Hall of Fame/ Mike Bolt
Page 36: HHOF Images, Hockey Hall of Fame/Josh Holmberg
Page 52: HHOF-IIHF Images, Hockey Hall of Fame-International Hockey/ Dan Hamilton
Page 68: HHOF-IIHF Images, Hockey Hall of Fame-International Hockey/ Matthew Manor
Page 84: HHOF Images, Graphic Artists/ Photo Credit Unknown
Page 102: HHOF Images, Hockey Hall of Fame/Frank Prazak
Page 120: HHOF Images, Paul Bereswill/ Paul Bereswill
Page 136: HHOF Images, Portnoy/Lewis Portnoy
Page 154: HHOF-IIHF Images, Europhoto-Finland/Jani Rajamaki
Page 172: HHOF Images, Hockey Hall of Fame/No Photo Credit

BIBLIOGRAPHY

Bibliography: A list of on-line and printed references used for researching Fire on Ice.

Ammsa.com
Arkells.ca
Bigsixhockey.com
Breastfriends.ca
Brookslaich.com
But I Loved it Plenty Well, by Allen J. Abel
CBC.ca
City-data.com
Collegehockeyinc.com
Columbus Dispatch
Ducks.nhl.com
88 Years of Puck Chasing in Saskatchewan, by Brenda Zeman and Joe Zeman
ESPN.com
Flames.nhl.com
Globesports.com
Googlemaps.com
HHOF.com
Hartnellmacarthurgolfclassic.com
Hockeyandhearts.com
Hockeydb.com
Hockeydraftcentral.com
Hrf.sk.ca
Junior Hockey's Royal Franchise: The Regina Pats, by Darrell Davis and Ron Johnston
Justsportsstats.com

Melville Advance

Nativehockey.com

Neudorf1.sasktelwebhosting.com

NHL.com

Northernpride.ml.com

Regina.ca

Regina Leader-Post

Saskatchewan Sports Legends, by John Chaput

Saskatoon.ca

Saskatoon StarPhoenix

Saskhockeyhalloffame.com

SHA.sk.ca

Sportslistoftheday.com

Statcan.gc.ca

Stats.gov.sk.ca

Townofaltcoasts.ca

Townofstrasbourg.ca

Python Pothole Repair; University of California - Davis

Quanthockey.com

Rauzulusstreet.com

Ruhf.org

Shootingstarsfoundation.com

Sports Illustrated

Wawota.com

Wheatkings.com

Wickeddeadly.com

Wikipedia.com

Yukoncollege.yk.ca